Silver Link Silk Editions
SLP

By Rail to the Music Halls

David John Hindle MA

By Rail to the Music Halls

© David Hindle 2020

All rights reserved. No part of this publication may be reproduced, stored in a retrieval system or transmitted, in any form or by any means, electronic, mechanical, photocopying, recording or otherwise, without prior permission in writing from Silver Link Books, Mortons Media Group Ltd.

First published in 2020

British Library Cataloguing in Publication Data

A catalogue record for this book is available from the British Library.

ISBN 978 1 85794 541 6

Silver Link Books
Mortons Media Group Limited
Media Centre
Morton Way
Horncastle
LN9 6JR
Tel/Fax: 01507 529535

email: sohara@mortons.co.uk
Website: www.nostalgiacollection.com
Printed and bound in the Czech Republic

Rebuilt 'West Country' Class 'Pacific' No 34037 *Clovelly* passes the impressive Battledown Viaduct after Worting Junction with a Saturday Birmingham to Bournemouth train on 21 July 1962.

Silver Link Silk Editions
SLP

By Rail to the Music Halls

David John Hindle MA

Foreword by Gary Morecambe

SLP

A Silver Link Book

Contents

The Overture		6
The Prologue:	The evolution of music hall and railways	10
Reprise:	Legal considerations and four national treasures	25
Chapter One	Footplates and footlights	31
Chapter Two	The good old days? Charles Dickens catches a train during *Hard Times*	39
Chapter Three	Accolade: 'Maybe it's because I'm a Londoner'	42
Chapter Four	Frank Matcham: Theatre architect extraordinaire	52
Chapter Five	London's magnificent Coliseum	74
Chapter Six	The bread and butter circuit	76
Chapter Seven	Morecambe and Wise: Getting their act together on a train while touring the provinces	85
Chapter Eight	The rise of cinema and decline of music hall	94
Chapter Nine	'I do like to be beside the seaside'	103
Interval:	A gallery of steam trains	119
Chapter Ten	'All stations to Southport for a night out at the Garrick'	128
Chapter Eleven	By ship, steam train and horse-drawn tram to the Gaiety Theatre, Isle of Man	138
Chapter Twelve	Nine great British music halls and variety theatres	142
Chapter Thirteen	A potpourri of comic railway interludes	152
Encore:	'There's just time for one more verse of "Down at the Old Bull and Bush", followed by personal recollections	157
The Grand Finale:	All stations to the music hall by steam-hauled trains	161
Appendix One	Historiography	177
Appendix Two	The Matcham theatres	178
Acknowledgements and Bibliography		180
Index		184

Foreword by Gary Morecambe

Gary Morecambe with a portrait of Eric.

I look no further than my own father's experiences to illustrate the point: a 2nd Class train ride between Birmingham and Coventry in 1940 is not the most obvious starting point for the best-loved double act in British comedy history. The Second World War was well under way in 1940, but not for Morecambe and Wise. Fourteen-year-old Eric Bartholomew and his best friend Ernie Wiseman were travelling that day with my paternal grandmother, Eric's Mum and mentor, Sadie Bartholomew. The star-struck teenagers had been performing in a touring youth theatre as solo acts. As usual the boys were over-excited after the show, and going through their Abbot and Costello, Laurel and Hardy impressions. Sadie, who was trying to sleep, made a suggestion that would change showbiz history for ever.

'Why don't you two stop fooling around and put your minds to something else. Why not form a double act of your own?'

For over 20 years Morecambe and Wise learned their craft in Britain's variety theatres while travelling extensively throughout the country. When variety effectively died and many theatres went permanently dark in the 1950 and 1960s, they switched to television spectaculars, which were enjoyed by millions throughout the world.

This profusely illustrated narrative will offer something more than mere reading enjoyment. David's enthusiasm and expertise on music hall history is unbounded, and, in railway nomenclature, I give this publication the green light.

Gary Morecambe

David J. Hindle is an author and social historian with a particular interest in the genre of music hall and the history of the railways. In this, his latest book, he flags up parallels to be drawn with the origins of railways and music hall. This is an original concept, notwithstanding that long before the age of the automobile it was the railways that conveyed audiences and performers to the music halls that evolved to become variety theatres.

The Overture

This book is designed to appeal to devotees of unashamed nostalgia by combining the golden age of steam with the awesome Victorian music halls and variety theatres of the Edwardian era and early 20th century. As the railway expanded, theatres and music halls began to stage international performances on a lavish scale, increasingly served by the railway with improved mobility for scenery, costumes, animals and equipment.

The combination of railway and music hall history is well worthy of close scrutiny for the social historian. The Victorian and Edwardian music hall and its association with the first railways is relatively understudied. Nevertheless, the coming of the first music halls coincided with railway beginnings and are two of the most thought-provoking and important features of 19th-century social history.

The origin and demise of the music halls and variety theatres closely parallels the steam era, spanning about 140 years, beginning with George Stephenson's *Rocket* steam locomotive in 1829 and ending with the last British Railways steam locomotives in regular service, which were condemned to a siding and the cutter's torch on 4 August 1968. Likewise the period that begins with the first music hall in about 1832 ends with

Right: The original Empire Theatre, Edinburgh, was the first of the Moss Empire chain of theatres, opening in 1892. *Courtesy of Capital Theatres*

Far right: This grand old Scottish music hall is a rare survivor: the all-aglow Pavilion theatre, Glasgow. *Courtesy of Marie Donnelly*

The Overture

the closure of the last variety theatres in the mid-1960s.

By the mid- to late-19th century the first purpose-built music halls were being built in London. The emergence of a distinct music hall genre and style can be credited to a fusion of musical influences. The English music hall created a demand for new and catchy popular songs, and often the lyrics contained veiled references to sexual innuendo. However, Victorian England was an age of stuffy complacency, prudery and top-hatted hypocrisy, remembered for its crinolines and hansom cabs, satanic mills and streets with gas lamps and knocker-uppers, and for the birth of a peculiarly English institution – the music hall – often referred to as the good old days. But were they?

The legendary music hall performer Marie Lloyd sang the railway

By tramcar to Preston's Royal Hippodrome at the time of Marie Lloyd's visit to the theatre in 1911. *Courtesy of Linda Barton*

The appropriately named *Evening Star* was the last steam locomotive to be built for British Railways, marking the end of an era. *David Hindle*

song 'Oh! Mr Porter what shall I do? I want to go to Birmingham and they're taking me on to Crewe. Take me back to London as quickly as you can, Oh! Mr Porter what a silly girl I am.' Fortunately, however, she caught the right train when she topped the bill at Preston's Royal Hippodrome on 30 October 1911. The entire cast would have travelled by train before arriving at the next music hall on their tour.

The *Lancashire Post* gave a favourable report: 'Marie Lloyd

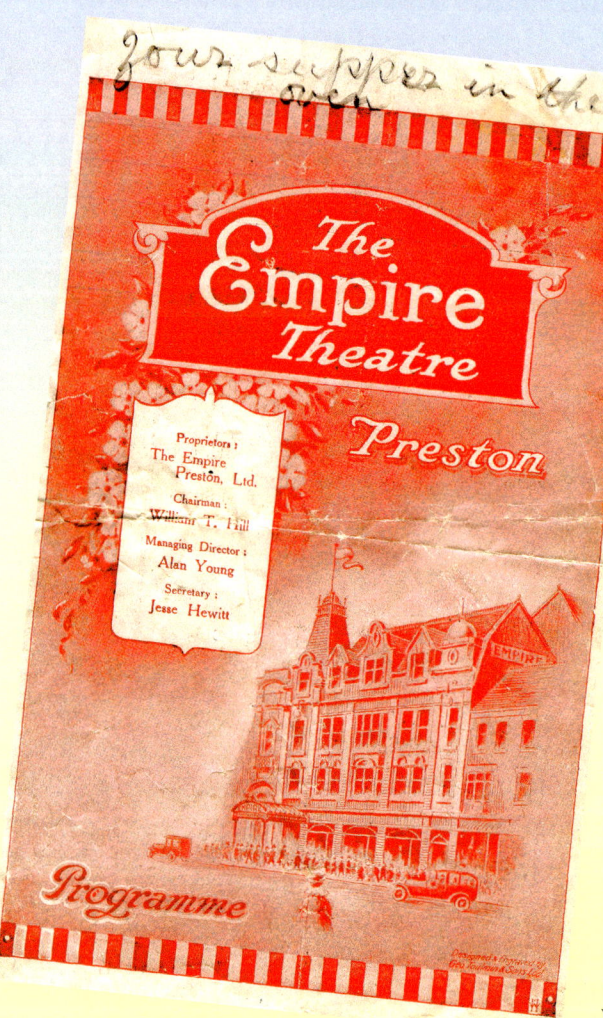

The quintessence of music hall was *Abov:* Marie Lloyd. Picture courtesy of Harrogate Royal Hall, where Marie Lloyd performed while touring England by rail.

Right: This Preston Empire Theatre variety programme dated 1924 is inscribed in pencil with the words 'your supper is in the oven', which suggests an irate spouse whose patience had run out and gone to bed. 'Get the habit, twice nightly.' *Author*

heads a capital bill of fare at the Hippodrome this week and had a flattering reception at the matinee yesterday afternoon and in the two evening performances, large audiences appearing to hear the Queen of Comediennes.' Lloyd evidently captured her audience with her double entendre and broad humour and was billed as the greatest success ever to play the Hippodrome. The generic supporting music hall cast was typical of those days, featuring a vocalist and dancer, an acrobatic comedian and a Houdini-style act billed 'Carl Mysto, the monarch of the manacles'.

Variety theatres and music halls capitalised on the advertising slogan 'Get the habit – Twice nightly', often emblazoned in neon lighting, to attract regular patrons with a choice of evening performances and a matinee. This concept was to increase profitability and make performances more convenient for families and shift workers. Those residing in rural parishes and villages would have

The Overture

been eager to catch a train into town to see the latest live shows. During 1924 Margaret Noblett paid a penny for a bar of Nestle's chocolate from the machine on Grimsargh station before catching the train to Preston to meet her friends and see a music hall performance at the old Empire Theatre on Church Street. Music hall visits were social events attended by the family, friends and work colleagues.

Today variety and music hall survive but only as uncomfortable revivals of the real thing. Moreover, the rebirth of preserved steam locomotives is now of interest to those wanting to experience the magic of the steam age.

The diverse origins of music hall incorporated elements from wide-ranging forms of entertainment, including circus. Throughout this book I include colour photographs of the great Regency, Victorian and Edwardian theatres of Britain, most of which would have featured music hall. At the same time I hope to raise the profile and public awareness of some of the prettiest theatres in Britain. Also featured are photographs by leading railway photographers, depicting the glory years of the steam locomotive era. Countless memories have inspired research and provided the stimulation to share a measure of England's social history.

'Writing a book is an adventure. To begin with it is a toy and an amusement, then it becomes a mistress, and then it becomes a master and then a tyrant. The last phase is that just as you are about to be reconciled to your servitude, you kill the monster, and fling him out to the public.'
Winston Churchill

Howard and Wyndham's Royal Court Theatre, Liverpool, staged old time music hall in the 1960s, starring Hylda Baker and a real veteran of the genre, Hetty King. *Author*

The Prologue: The evolution of music hall and railways

'*Ladies and Gentlemen – it now gives me the greatest pleasure to introduce for your evening's delectation the finest and most delectable, the most rousing and riotous scintillating entertainment, the one, the one and only Music Hall. Positively to placate academia I begin with how it all began.*'

I begin by defining music hall and variety theatres. The Oxford English Dictionary defines music hall as a hall used for musical performances, a hall licensed for singing, dancing and other entertainments exclusive of dramatic performances.

'Variety' can be defined as a series of attractions or 'turns' unconnected by any theme, and was a term more associated with the 20th century as a similar form of entertainment that grew out of music hall. Variety was better packaged when presented to its audiences, and later took advantage of the popularity of jazz, dance music and revue. In Great Britain variety was originally known as music hall, though the two terms are often used interchangeably. In the first music halls patrons would be seated at a table in the auditorium and could drink alcohol and smoke tobacco while watching the show, the entertainment being ancillary to the alcohol. In a theatre, by contrast, the audience was seated in a properly constructed auditorium with a separate bar-room where alcohol was ancillary to the entertainment.

Music hall has its origin with street ballad singers, public house singing saloons, travelling fairs and circus-inspired acts. Significantly, the beginnings of railways coincide with the emergence of singing saloons, circus and music hall during the 1830s and '40s. Among the attractions on tour by rail were heavyweight lifters, ghost illusionists, boxing booths and marionettes, as well as the first cinematograph performances and menageries with daring lion tamers. Most travelling circuses held a promotional circus procession from the local railway station, where special trains conveyed acrobats, jugglers and strongmen as well as dogs, monkeys and even elephants.

Such was the popularity of circuses that you were as likely to see jugglers and aerial acts on a trip to the theatre or music hall as at a circus. An 1829 performance at the Theatre Royal, Preston, presented a comic spectacle between two plays, with two men, masquerading as monkeys around the gallery, before carrying out a daring circus escapade from gallery to stage. Trapeze wires were strung from the ceiling of Preston's Theatre Royal on 14 September 1861. The famous tightrope walker, 'Blondin', starred high above the crowds in the stalls, illustrating the ongoing popularity of circus performers throughout the 19th century with all social groups.[1] The foregoing are examples of how audiences were being drawn towards the culture of music hall in the established theatre. The late Victorian era saw the touring circus attracting international productions with famous names, and its immense popularity was reflected by the growing audiences and continuing high admission prices coinciding with the peak time for music hall growth.

Newsome's Circus was situated alongside Preston's East Lancashire (Butler Street) station. The circus and convenient station location, together with a special suburban

The Prologue: The evolution of music hall and railways

train service, was duly advertised in the *Preston Guardian* on 3 July 1872:

'Newsome's Grand Circus – adjoining the railway station, Butler Street, Preston. Immense success of last night's Cinderella: notice to the inhabitants of Longridge, Goosnargh, Fulwood and neighbourhood, a special train will leave tomorrow, Thursday evening at a quarter to eleven, for the accommodation of parties from that locality visiting the circus'.

The name 'OHMY' was derived from its proprietor Joseph Smith, who, as a circus bungee jumper, was in the habit of shouting 'oh my!', and this led to the naming of his travelling circus.[2]

In 1945 Harry Pye documented his recollections of late Victorian circuses and Buffalo Bill's Wild West Show, which visited Preston by special trains: 'The memories of exciting entertainment, as for instance Buffalo Bill's gigantic Wild West Show, housed in immense and numerous canvas erections on the Penwortham Holme and then, in later years, the enterprising Barnum and Bailey combinations on the same site.'

Buffalo Bill's (real name William Cody) Wild West Show made several visits to Britain in the first decade of the 20th century. The logistics of these British tours illustrate how the railways were indispensable in the cause of spectacular entertainment. Three trains pulled a total of 150 carriages around the country visiting many cities and towns, and Preston was on the itinerary. The trains carried tons of scenery, a portable arena, props and lighting equipment. When the British tours ended, the Wild West Show returned to the USA, sailing from Liverpool to New York.

From a gin palace to a King's palace

Embryonic music halls were originally tavern rooms, singing saloons and even gin palaces, which provided entertainment for their patrons in the form of music and specialty acts. Throughout Britain music hall entertainment became increasingly popular with audiences, so much so that numerous public houses built adjacent annexes that were designed so that patrons could consume food and alcohol and smoke tobacco in the auditorium while the entertainment took place. The developing music halls were also termed singing rooms, concert rooms and concert halls.

Until the railways were established it was difficult and expensive for actors and music hall performers to tour the provincial halls. In time-honoured fashion the venerable Chairman began to introduce clog dancers, sand dancers, musicians, ballad and operatic singers, jugglers, ventriloquists, clowns, serio-comics (having both serious and comedic qualities or tendencies) and circus-inspired novelty acts, male and female impersonators, lions comiques (a caricature of upper-class toffs or swells), mime artists, impressionists, trampoline acts and comic pianists. All represented the range of generic acts that audiences could expect to see in the music halls of Britain throughout the Victorian era.

In Lancashire, the home of the cotton barons and a burgeoning textile industry during the Industrial Revolution, Thomas Sharples opened one of the country's first established music halls at Bolton in 1832 and called it the Bolton Star Music Hall. The *Bolton Guardian* reported that the Star Music Hall had a plain stage and to the left the chairman's box. Mr Geoghegan, the manager, acted as Chairman and he had a mallet and called out the names of the performers. Performances began at 7.30 each night, and the curtain was wound up by hand. A well-known character named 'Museum Jack' lit the lamps and footlights with a taper and played the piano. If a turn failed to please, Mr Geoghegan said, 'You're no good,' and ejected the hapless performer. There were 2d and 4d checks or tokens (known as wet money in exchange for alcohol); these were small coins bearing the inscription of a laurel leaf and a seven-point star.

At Preston the pioneering although decadent venue, Albion Singing Saloon, Clarke's Yard, Church Street, was opened in 1839. This was the same year that the local Longridge branch line was completed, commensurate with the birth of the railway network in north-west England.

In his 1842 Annual Report, Prison Chaplain the Reverend John Clay provides evidence of three early Preston concert halls: 'One of the concert rooms, capable of holding 650 persons, was opened in the summer of 1839. Two others of smaller dimension were opened in the spring of 1841.'[3] Accordingly were born Preston's first established concert halls, beginning with the Albion Concert Hall in 1839. With two additional halls in 1841, a pattern of growth and evidence of commercialisation and regularity of the industry begins to emerge.[4] The Albion became popular with the working classes of both sexes and some members of the lower middle class, as well as clerks and lawyers. Although audience composition varied between halls, it nevertheless remained integral to working class culture, and was especially popular with young textile workers. This can be attributed in part to the audiences' need to be distracted from the hardships of employment in the mills, and the instigation of a shorter working week introduced by the Factories Act of 1850.

Music hall was born in London thanks to the father of the halls, Charles Morton, in December 1849. Morton gave concert performances on three nights a week at the Canterbury Arms, Lambeth, though this was not the first music hall. Indeed, searching for the very first London music hall is like searching for the Holy Grail! Whatever the arguments, archetypal elements of the old music hall industry have vanished forever. The first primitive

This illustration portrays a room that is not purpose-built but a prototype music hall with piano accompaniment and a low dais provided, as well as the convivial Chairman. *Courtesy of Bob Gregson*

yet flamboyant singing saloons and pub music halls of Lancashire's textile towns were probably the first in England. Bolton and Preston were both cotton towns, at the forefront of national music hall growth, with the Bolton Star music hall opening in 1832 and Preston's Albion music hall in 1839.

The Preston model might be considered to be a microcosm of a national pattern for the development of music hall, beginning with 'free and easies' where a group of friends would meet to drink and hear songs, and ranging to the professional, commodious and splendidly decorated variety theatres of the late Victorian and Edwardian eras, though the town had its own unique characteristics.

Music hall began with the free and easy singing room characterised by a group of amateurs singing round a piano. Throughout the Lancashire textile towns there were modified rooms in public houses and beer houses and separate harmonic rooms. This marks the start of professionalism, with regular concerts in a separate room.

In Lancashire cotton towns music halls progressed to become large purpose-built rooms, linked with the pub or as a separate annex, and by the 1860s the term music hall was increasingly recognised, though such premises were still named concert rooms in certain press reports. Indeed, it became difficult to distinguish between music halls and popular theatres. At Preston, Edward Blackoe opened the 'George Concert Room' on Saturday 29 November 1864:

'Edward Blackoe of the "George Inn", Friargate, intends to open a new and very extensive concert room, built expressly for the purpose… First-class talent has been engaged and nothing will be wanted to make entertainment pleasing, happy and comfortable, so that even the most fastidious may go and spend a few jovial hours to their heart's content.'[5]

More than 1,000 patrons attended the opening night and Blackoe proclaimed:

'This is living proof that the people of this town will support entertainments when they are of a good and respectable character. The hall will be opened every evening about seven o'clock and closed about ten.'[6]

A later development phase of the Victorian music hall. This sort of pub activity generated between the 1840s and the 1860s can be seen as the birth of music hall, a pattern that grew during successive decades and climaxed with the lavish British variety theatres of the late Victorian era. *Courtesy of Bob Gregson*

At the George:

'There was nothing calculated to disgust or demoralise… The curtain rose and the usual concert-hall swell, dressed in loud and utterly impossible attire, came upon the stage. In one corner sat a rubicund-looking Chairman who announced the coming man… After a well-merited encore the curtain fell and the orchestra played selections until the Chairman announced another singer.'[7]

The presence of a Chairman and formalised programming is further evidence of the music hall genre and its greater level of organisation.

John Blackoe was obviously convinced of the demand for popular entertainment, as he followed his brother's lead when he opened the New King's Head Concert Hall, Preston, on 14 November 1870, claiming it to be the largest and most respectable concert hall in town.[8] These halls were designed chiefly so that people could consume food and alcohol and smoke tobacco in the auditorium while the entertainment took place.

Comedy, in a variety of styles, was a vital part of the evolutionary music hall repertoire, with serio-comics featuring prominently.

Early concert hall songs

Another key figure to emerge in Preston music hall was the singer, whether he or she was a comic, a duettist, a sentimental balladeer or an operatic singer. While popular songs could help draw the working-class audience, there is some evidence of a broad musical culture in music hall, especially so at the Sun Inn, where an operatic vocalist appeared in 1870. The playing of sacred music at the Wagon & Horses on Sunday evenings during 1861 fostered a respectable religious image.

The musical forms most associated with music hall evolved in part from traditional folk songs and songs written for popular drama, becoming by the 1850s a distinct musical style. Subject matter became more contemporary and humorous, and accompaniment was provided by larger house orchestras. There was more public access to commercial entertainment and to a wider range of musical instruments as well as the piano. The consequent change in musical taste from traditional to more professional forms of entertainment arose in response to the rapid industrialisation at the time of the Industrial Revolution.

The first music hall songs often promoted the alcoholic wares of the owners of the halls in which they were performed. The first major music hall song success was 'Champagne Charlie' (1867), which had a major influence in establishing the new art form. 'Champagne Charlie'

The opening of the mid-Victorian King's Head Concert Hall, Preston, and a period programme typical of the music hall genre. Author

was composed by Alfred Lee with lyrics by George Leybourne, and premiered in August 1866 at the Princess Concert Hall in Leeds. Accordingly, by the 1870s the songs were free of their folk music origins, and particular songs also started to become associated with particular singers. 'Champagne Charlie' would have been sung in pub music halls.

Music hall songs could be romantic, patriotic at the time of the First World War, humorous or sentimental as the need arose. The Clarence Music Hall was one of Preston's last concert rooms to close. A programme printed in about 1883 mentions the Preston North End football song and Belger, one of the team's players. The programme also illustrates the moderate style of locally based entertainment on offer and claims that 'It was the place to spend a convivial hour', as a drop in to sample the programme. Curiously, 'children in arms were not admitted unless brought by someone.'

Music hall developed into purpose-built variety theatres in the late 1870s, with the bars separated from the auditorium. 'The theatre is now enriched with comfortable tip-up seats and padded gallery benches. They are no longer brilliantly lit rooms where friends meet to drink and listen to a song. They are theatres where audiences assemble to be entertained.'[9]

Peering over the balcony, or 'the gods'.
Courtesy of Bob Gregson

Preston's George Music Hall was a precursor to the new Gaiety Palace Theatre of Varieties, Tithebarn Street, Preston, with a capacity for 2,000 patrons. It was purpose-built and detached from the pub, with fixed pit and gallery seats and a properly equipped stage. The Gaiety was the town's first substantial Victorian variety theatre opening in 1882 and as such was a great influence on the evolution of local music hall. By now the Chairman had long disappeared from variety theatres. The acts were identified by the sequence of acts in numerical order on a lighted panel on either side of the proscenium, corresponding with the programme. In appearance it anticipated the Edwardian variety theatres with its curving balconies, rows of seats, large stage and proscenium arch.

The tradition of music hall being a working-class male preserve was beginning to change, for there is some evidence that respectable families were being attracted to the Gaiety during 1884, and a high level of discipline was apparent at Preston's Gaiety Music Hall: 'Police in attendance and strict order enforced.' Female attendance was encouraged, but prostitutes were discouraged by the inducement of 'Thursday nights – ladies free if accompanied by a gentleman but children must be paid for.'[10] The general rule was that any unaccompanied woman in a public place was a prostitute.

Music halls were suspect because of the presence of prostitutes. Here middle-class men could meet working-class women, who

The opening variety show at the Gaiety coincided with Preston Guild celebrations in September 1882. *Author*

Below: The former Gaiety Theatre, Preston, awaits demolition. *Courtesy of Lancashire Evening Post*

would often be prostitutes. To ensure the moral well-being of the public, police were instructed to be in attendance at the music hall. The variety bill included a caveat that stated 'No ladies admitted unless accompanied by gentlemen' in an effort to eradicate the ladies of the night who had been practising their trade in the dark recesses of the gallery and balcony.

Towards the end of the Victorian era women of all classes gained more autonomy in the pursuit of leisure. Oral history testaments indicate that women often travelled from suburban and out-of-town areas to attend the theatre during the afternoon.

The opening of the Gaiety marks a significant point in the progress of music hall, but it does not show that it was atypical in matching the national trend. Only six years later, in October 1888, the Gaiety ceased to present music hall and switched to drama.

Following a serious fire in 1900 the theatre was renamed the Princes Theatre. The Preston-born cinema impresario Will Onda (real name Hugh Rain) played a key role in cinema provision in the town, and by 1913 the Princes Theatre began to present films.

Paradoxically, Preston, a town that, in other respects, broadly follows the national and regional trends in music hall development, had no music hall provision during the 1890s, evidenced by a reduction in music and dancing licences and archived records. A combination of factors – for example the newly formed Preston North End Football team – seems to have led to a temporary hiatus of music hall, which forestalled syndicate interest during the 1890s.

However, this music hall void was filled when William Henry Broadhead extended his syndicate of music halls based in Manchester to Preston, with the building of the Royal Hippodrome in 1905. The type of enthusiasm generated for the opening indicates that Broadhead was fulfilling a definite need. According to the press, comments were made that 'It certainly filled a long-felt gap in the town's entertainment provision.'

Preston's music hall patrons

The Prologue: The evolution of music hall and railways

were adequately catered for with the provision of the huge King's Palace Variety Theatre, in February 1913. The period from 1905 represents a second music hall boom, when famous music hall stars graced the stage of all three of Preston's variety theatres during the golden years of variety.

Music hall ended, arguably, after the First World War when halls renamed their entertainment as variety. Variety had always been an alternative name for the music hall, but it gradually became associated with a distinctive form of entertainment. Family entertainment saw sketches become part of the repertoire, together with progressive changes in styles of entertainment. This rise of music hall sketches broadened the social base of the public for variety entertainment.

Again, reflecting the national picture, Preston's music hall industry was consigned to the annals of social history during the 1950s.

Finally, Professor John Walton reaffirms:

'What emerges is the sheer extent and range of commercial entertainment provision in the late Victorian and Edwardian cotton towns of Lancashire, building on and expanding from mid-Victorian foundations, and reaching almost all levels of working-class society.'[11]

By period steam train to the music hall
Matching the developing music halls, this section puts the spotlight on railways from their humble beginnings in 1829 to the mid-20th century, when steam locomotives ruled the permanent way.

On 27 September 1825 the first steam engine took to the tracks of the Stockton & Darlington Railway. It was designed by George Stephenson and proudly carried the appropriate name of *Locomotion*. The Liverpool & Manchester Railway officially opened in 1830 and was the first commercial passenger railway to operate in north-west England. Thereafter railway mania was to impact on Preston, and indeed the rest of the world. Railways and trains have featured in hundreds of music hall songs. In 1846 a music hall song entitled 'Railway Mania', composed by James Briton, appeared at the height of the so-called mania of the 1840s. The term indicates the utter frenzy over rail construction during the mid-19th century.

The 1840s were by far the biggest decade for railway growth, and from the start they were used for excursion traffic. On 5 July 1841 32-year-old Thomas Cook engaged an excursion train to carry about 500 temperance supporters from Leicester to a meeting in Loughborough. The railways revolutionised travel and excursion traffic began the mass market for leisure. Railway

Furness Railway 0-4-0 No 3 *Coppernob* of 1846. *Courtesy of David Eaves*

A charming study of a Furness Railway steam-hauled train circling Morecambe Bay circa 1900. *Courtesy of Bob Gregson*

mania reached its zenith in 1846, when no fewer than 272 Acts of Parliament were enacted to set up new companies and thereby establishing new railways.

To illustrate the evolution and development of the nation's railways, in 1820 there were no commercial passenger railways in Britain, but by 1912 the landscape had been transformed with 120 companies operating more than 20,000 miles of track. Co-existing with the music hall, the railway network of the North West was more or less complete by 1850, and included part of the Anglo-Scottish route between London Euston and Glasgow, nowadays known as the West Coast Main Line.

Nationally the age of railways really

Early days on the Lancaster & Carlisle Railway (today's West Coast Main Line) with a train crossing Eamont Viaduct. The Lancaster & Carlisle Railway extended the line over Shap to reach Carlisle in 1846 and Glasgow in 1848. Before that an important route to Scotland was via the Fleetwood-Ardrossan Ferry. *Courtesy of Bob Gregson*

The Prologue: The evolution of music hall and railways

got under way around 1870. At the same time there grew up a chain of large well-equipped variety theatres served by the railway network, to accommodate touring productions and famous names of the music hall stage.

The late 19th century was the apotheosis of Victorian music hall, and by this time the railways too were becoming fast and well organised. This accessibility of music hall to hundreds of towns and cities is exemplified by an article in the *Lancashire Evening Post* dated 15 October 1896, describing the new West Coast Express train with only four stops:

'Yesterday a new fast express on the West Coast route commenced running from Euston to Aberdeen, leaving London at 10.15pm and stopping only at Crewe (156 miles), Carlisle (290 miles), Stirling and Perth. The initial run was in every respect satisfactory, as the express, which is now the fastest regular train on the north-west system, reached Carlisle at 3.56am, or 5 minutes ahead of time. The distance between London and Carlisle had thus been covered, with one stoppage only, in 5 hours 40 minutes, as compared with 5 hours 50 minutes by the other two night expresses on the same route to the north. There were four vehicles on the train well filled with passengers. The engine that ran from Crewe to Carlisle was the London & North Western No 2102 *Caradoc*, while the journey from Carlisle to Perth was accomplished by the Caledonian engine No 134. Although the new express did some fast running, its speed was not nearly equal to that obtained during last year's 'race', when the quickest time between Euston and Carlisle on the night of August 22-23 was 4 hours 36 minutes. The 105 miles from Wigan to Carlisle, which had been traversed by the 8pm express from Euston recently in 106 minutes, fell a long way behind the racing record of last August, when the maximum average speed between London and Carlisle reached 65 miles and 69 chains per hour.'

An article in the *Lancashire Daily Post* illustrates the healthy state of the above railway in 1896:

'The London & North Western Railway celebrates its [50-year] jubilee distinction today. A number of the lines of which it is composed were in operation more than fifty years ago, and notably the one between Liverpool and Manchester, but the company takes its consolidation from 16 July 1846. The company has about 60,000 employees, its permanent way extends to 1,900

Caledonian Railway No 434 at Carlisle. *Courtesy of Bob Gregson*

miles, and it has 3,000 engines, 5,000 passengers and 60,000 wagons, besides fleets of steamers and vast possessions in land and buildings. Careful management has brought the company to great prosperity, far beyond the dreams of the founders of our railway system, and the directors and other officials who are celebrating the jubilee with a dinner are entitled to speak with elation, enthusiasm and success of the London & North Western Railway.'

There is little doubt that the excursion train added to the cultural life

Class 'K1' LMS No 10131, formerly FR No 120, at Carnforth. *Courtesy of Bob Gregson*

LNWR No 5050 *Merrie Carlisle* at Penrith. *Courtesy of Bob Gregson*

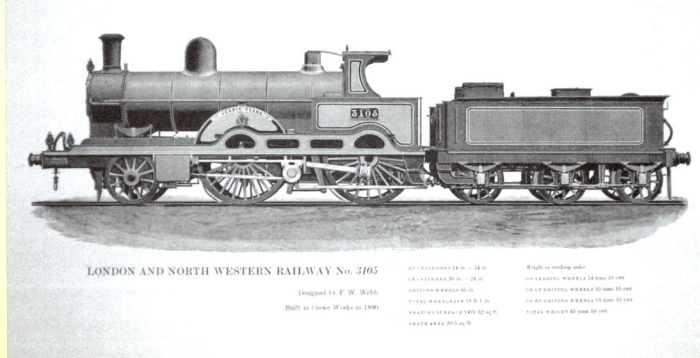

Above: LNWR No 3105 *Jeanie Deans. Courtesy of Bob Gregson*

Left: Furness Railway No 36 near Grange-over-Sands circa 1900. *Courtesy of Bob Gregson*

The Prologue: The evolution of music hall and railways

Lytham, Southport and Morecambe. The British railway poster came of age in 1923, following the Grouping of the many railway companies into the 'Big Four'. Each company advertised its routes through posters and brochures with the emphasis on seaside resorts and places rich in scenic grandeur and heritage, as well as resorts and cities offering a range of cultural interests. Leading poster artists were employed to persuade passengers to travel by train.

An LMS poster promoting Llandudno. *Courtesy of Bob Gregson*

'By Rail to the Music Halls'
The LMS issued combined rail and theatre tickets to several resorts. Here is an inclusive show at the Pier Pavilion, Llandudno. *Courtesy of Bob Gregson*

of the country both locally and nationally. Since mid-Victorian times excursions trains have enhanced people's lives with day or evening visits to towns, cities and seaside resorts and with the option of going to a show.

With an established railway network by 1870 the number of excursions increased dramatically, with crowds of people travelling to Lancashire's mainstream seaside resorts of Blackpool, Fleetwood,

By Rail to the Music Halls

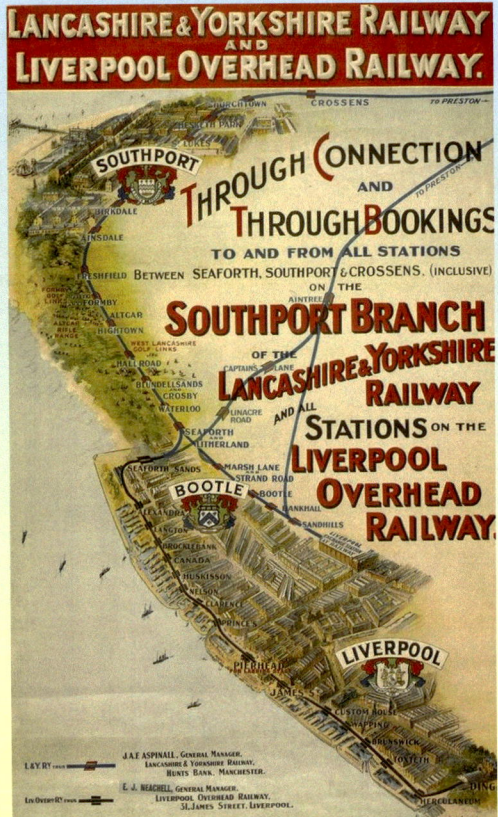

Above: The Liverpool Overhead Railway served the Empire and other city theatres.
Courtesy of Bob Gregson

Right: Leaving Whitby: perhaps passengers had visited the Whitby Pavilion Theatre, built in 1878.
Courtesy of Bob Gregson

By tramcar to the music hall

By the end of the Victorian era, and as the variety theatre became more elaborate and attractive to families, theatres were able to attract national stars to regional, local and seaside venues, many of whom were to travel by suburban rail services and tram to the theatre. The first tramcars and omnibuses were an important stimulus to the social and economic development of the outer suburbs of towns and cities. The music hall star George Lashwood sang a corny little ditty about riding on the top of a tramcar, and one wonders where he got his inspiration from! The extensive tramway network and suburban railway

network meant increased mobility for passengers throughout Britain. Electric trams ran hither and thither until finally reaching the end of the line, with bus substitution, which was a gradual process throughout the towns and cities of Britain. The last of the old traditional trams to be manufactured at English Electric, Preston, were dispatched to Aberdeen in 1940.

Blackpool Corporation Transport Department had the first urban electric tramway in the country when it opened in September 1885, since when the distinctive fleet has taken millions of holidaymakers to the town's variety theatres and centres of entertainment.

Tramcars outside the Bristol Hippodrome (*left*) and (*above*) the Palace Theatre, Manchester.

By Rail to the Music Halls

Above: A Preston tramcar outside the Empire Theatre, Church Street: 'Oh hello, Flossy – never mind the trams, good show at the Empire tonight!' *Author*

Right: By tramcar to the legendary Blackpool Tower: Blackpool Corporation vintage trams and buses. *Courtesy of Paul Atchinson*

Above and far right: Examples of early drama houses now long gone – the Theatre Royal, Manchester, and Manchester's Midland Hotel Theatre. The latter hotel was built by the Midland Railway to serve Manchester Central station, its northern terminus for rail services to London St Pancras. The luxurious hotel had a 1,000-seat purpose-built theatre where one of the first repertory companies in the country was established. *Courtesy of Bob Gregson*

Reprise: Legal considerations and three national treasures

It this section we focus on the relevant legislation governing music hall and its distinction from the legitimate theatre, and conclude with three examples of theatres that once rivalled music hall.

The Theatres Act 1843 introduced theatre regulation throughout the country for a growing entertainment industry. The legislation presented proprietors of theatres and small music saloons with a legal dilemma, as it distinguished between the legitimate drama house and music hall. The music halls were denied the freedom of staging drama, but were allowed the running sale and consumption of drink and tobacco in the auditorium. Proprietors could apply for a Lord Chamberlain's Licence, which authorised plays, or operate with a Liquor Licence issued by magistrates for the sale of drink and the provision of live entertainment. The 1843 Act thus demarcated music hall as a genre and formalised its economic link with alcohol. The Act removed the traditional, or legitimate, theatre's monopoly. Anyone could apply for a licence and present anything except drama in licensed premises.

Under the new Act, 'stage play'

Manchester. Midland Hotel. The Theatre.

was defined in broad terms to include tragedy, comedy, farce, opera, burlesque, revue, melodrama, pantomime, or other entertainment. Thus a distinction was drawn between stage plays and concert hall entertainment. Breaches of the Act were rare, as it was not until the 1870s, with the introduction of sketches into music hall, that there were grounds for complaint by legitimate theatre managers.

Nationally, the trend towards reform can be seen in two Select Committee reports of 1852 and 1877, which enquired into the licensing of pubs, beer houses, theatres and public places of entertainment, advocating closer police supervision, and expressing concerns over public morality.

A crude striptease sketch, staged in Preston's Albion Concert Hall, in 1850 was probably unlawful. The following piece describes the features of the hall, audience composition and seating capacity and the level of debauchery that probably hastened closure:

'The singing room is oblong about 30 yards by 10 yards and capable of holding, with the galleries, from 800 to 1,000 persons. One end is fitted up as a stage. The bar where the liquors are sold is placed in the middle. This gallery was occupied by the young of both sexes, from 14 years and upwards. The last piece performed was the "Spare Bed". He took off his coat and waistcoat, unbuttoned his braces, and commenced unbuttoning the waistband of his trousers, casting mock-modest glances around him; finally he took his trousers off and got into bed. Tremendous applause followed this act'[12]

Significantly the Albion attracted '500 to 600, mostly young people, factory people, lawyers, clerks and all sorts of people.'

Music hall ladies – I think not!
Courtesy of Bob Gregson

Legalistic intervention at Preston brought the Preston Improvement Act 1880, thereby effectively contributing to the curtailment of the pub music hall by reforming licensing procedures in respect of live entertainment. In Preston this element of driving music halls out of business was influenced by temperance campaigners seeking reform of liquor licensing legislation. Elsewhere in the provinces a similar trend of local acts affecting the existence of the pub music halls gradually followed suit. For example, Leicester's Chief Constable was granted a local act in 1884 to govern music licensing, and by 1885 the pub music hall had been virtually abolished.[13]

Throughout England the decline of the pub concert hall coincided with tighter controls on licensing brought about by the effect of the Metropolitan Management and Building Act 1878, governing building and safety regulations. The statute sought to prevent theatre fires; there were 87 instances of theatre fires in the United Kingdom between 1850 and 1900, some of which involved fatalities.

The Act, adopted nationally, required a Certificate of Suitability for a proscenium wall, dividing the stage from the auditorium, and a heavy iron safety curtain, but smaller concert halls could not take the weight. The economy of the halls was also seriously affected by a requirement that bars be separated from the auditoria with a consequential reduction in alcohol consumption. The new legislation caused some 200 halls to close, unable to meet the new standards.[14] According to Kift, building directives imposed on the proprietors of music halls 'were not so much intended to make the premises safe as to drive them out of business.'[15]

What has been shown is that the implementation of increased licensing laws, building regulations and temperance reform effectively curtailed the mid-Victorian music hall industry. Overall, this prompted some critics to denounce theatre legislation as an attempt to deprive the working classes of their pleasures. It led to decreasing audience participation and intimacy, tending to reduce the popular appeal and atmosphere of the older music halls.

Four national treasures
In contrast to the tawdry concert halls of yesteryear, we now journey to four national treasures that greatly differed from the genre of music hall and reflected their own brand of culture with actor managers touring the nation's theatres. Entertainment styles were many and varied and incorporated the first cinemas, which rivalled music hall. Moreover, all of this continued to be served by the golden age of steam railways.

The Royal Opera House, Covent Garden, London, is the third theatre to occupy the same site since 1732, the first two having been destroyed by fire. During the Second World War it was used as a Mecca dance hall, but after the war the idea of public subsidy of the arts was accepted. The decision was made to establish the Royal Opera House as the permanent year-round home of the opera and ballet companies, now known as the Royal Opera and the Royal Ballet. It was the ballet company that reopened the building on 20 February 1946 with *The Sleeping Beauty*.

The Royal Opera continues to invite the world's greatest artists and distinguished maestros to perform at Covent Garden. In recent years it has given an average of 150 performances per season, September-July, of approximately 20 operas, nearly half of these being new productions.

The façade, foyer and auditorium date from 1858, but almost

The magnificent Royal Opera House, with its grand classical portico facing Bow Street, was built in 1858.

every other element of the present complex dates from an extensive reconstruction in the 1990s. The main auditorium seats 2,256 people in four tiers, and is a Grade I listed building.

The Old Vic is a 1,000-seat theatre located near the South Bank, Lambeth, south London. It was first established in 1818 as the Royal Coburg Theatre. Astonishingly, in 1824 the Shakespearean actor Edmund Kean addressed the audience during his curtain call saying,

The Old Vic, London, is a national treasure. *Photos courtesy of Manuel Harlan*

'I have never acted to such a set of ignorant, unmitigated brutes as I see before me.' The theatre was taken over by Emma Cons in 1880 (who is commemorated with a plaque outside the theatre), and formally named the Royal Victoria Hall, although by this time it was already known as the 'Old Vic.'

Under Laurence Olivier it became the National Theatre of Great Britain on its formation in 1963, and the National Theatre remained at the Old Vic until new premises were constructed on the South Bank, opening in 1976.

The theatre celebrated its 200th birthday on Friday 11 May 2018. This acclaimed theatre has brought high art to multitudes of theatregoers and has witnessed many dramatic moments, transformations and changes of ownership over three centuries. Nevertheless, it is a people's theatre and gives a real sense of

Reprise: Legal considerations and three national treasures

The Theatre Royal, Bury St Edmunds and its splendid Regency interior.

what Victorian theatre was like. Today it is designated as a Grade II listed building and survives as a national treasure.

The Theatre Royal, Bury St Edmunds was designed and built in 1819 by William Wilkins. It is one of one of the most intimate and historic theatres in Britain and a superb example of a Regency playhouse. At that time it would certainly have enjoyed large audiences, particularly as the local community would not have been able to travel far for entertainment until the arrival of the railway in the 1840s.

The theatre has endured a chequered history, and it was in 1965 that it reopened after years of neglect and was vested in the National Trust a decade later. Between 2005 and 2007 it was renovated and restored to its Regency origins. Dame Judi Dench CBE said, 'The Theatre Royal Bury St Edmunds holds a unique place in the history of theatre in this country as well as a special place in my heart.'

The Theatre Royal, Brighton installed gas lighting in around 1819, one of the first theatres in the country to do so. Interestingly, a spotlight effect was created by burning a piece of lime in the flame,

One of the top five oldest working theatres in the country, Brighton's Theatre Royal is today a Grade II listed building with an illustrious history. It opened on 27 June 1807 with a performance of Shakespeare's *Hamlet*.

resulting in a bright white light, and this is the origin of the phrase 'in the limelight', referring to a star or, more broadly, anyone at the centre of attention.

The theatre struggled until it was purchased in 1854 by actor Henry John Nye Chart, who engaged theatre architect Charles Phipps to begin a programme of expansion and redevelopment. Phipps would go on to become a celebrated architect with numerous high-profile buildings to his name, including at least 25 provincial theatres and almost a dozen in London. His contribution to the Theatre Royal at Brighton was enormous. He literally raised the roof by creating the three, closely spaced balconies that give the auditorium such unusual intimacy, pushing the capacity to a colossal 1,900, almost double what it is today.

In 1920 the financial buoyancy of the theatre enabled the directors to buy adjacent properties and make substantial improvements to the building. In the middle and later 20th century the Royal's stature and national reputation continued to grow. The Redgrave family, Laurence Olivier, John Gielgud, Charlton Heston, Margot Fonteyn, Rex Harrison and Judi Dench all performed there.

In 1984 London impresario David Land bought the theatre and subsidised productions out of his own pocket up to £400,000 a year. Land, and later his son Brook, ran the theatre for a decade and a half, revitalising the Royal with popular acts. In 1999 the theatre was bought by the Ambassador Theatre Group and a full-scale modernisation scheme commenced. There is tremendous visual evidence of the theatre's growth, giving it almost unparalleled character, which is what makes this historic building so unique.

Chapter One – Footplates and Footlights

It was a new division of work and leisure that began to emerge in the Industrial Revolution with the coming of the railway network, coinciding with the emergence and growth of the music hall industry. The effect of the railways on popular entertainment meant greater mobility, not only for the public but also for the London-based touring companies. Productions were now able to penetrate the provinces by steam train, conveying the famous and not so famous to their ultimate destination. In the mid-19th century it was the railways that changed everything. From a social perspective this newly found mobility lured the public to the very first music halls long before the dawn of the automobile. For about 75 years the railways were the only form of proper land transport. Trains have now perhaps lost their importance in that respect, but they still remain important to audiences and performers.

The charm of rural branch lines once epitomised those wonderful days of steam in a forgotten scenario of quaint little trains in a vanishing natural landscape. The branch lines provided new horizons for all classes of people. Travellers from far and wide enjoyed the coming of the first music

Right: Period steam locomotives: a historic photo of newly rebuilt 'Royal Scot' 4-6-0 No 6135 *The East Lancashire Regiment* at its naming ceremony at Preston station in 1947. *Courtesy of Douglas Willacy*

Below: New unrebuilt No 6100 *Royal Scot. Courtesy of Bob Gregson*

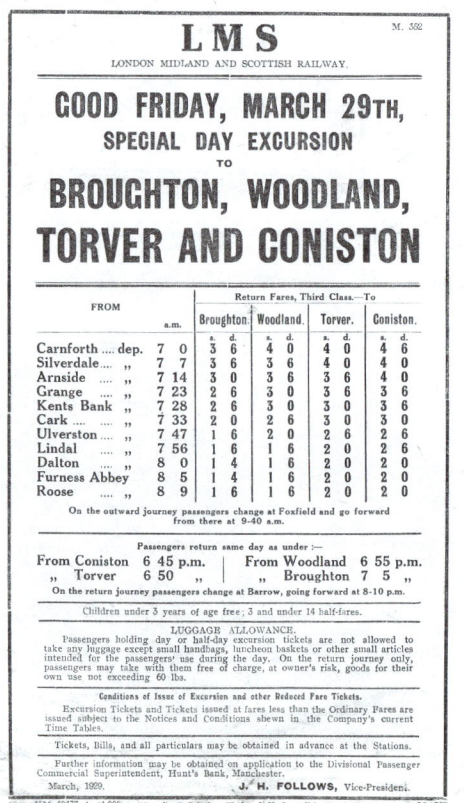

halls, cinemas and circuses to the region.

An article in *The Railway Magazine* in 1912 details the theatrical traffic carried on the LNWR on 22 October. A total of 112 theatrical companies were conveyed on the railway, comprising 2,374 passengers, 182 scenery trucks, and eight horse boxes.

During 1912 special trains conveyed the following companies, who

An LMS Special Day Excursion to Coniston in 1929. *Courtesy of Bob Gregson*

Top: The stunning station at Coniston nestles below Coniston Old Man on 17 May 1946. *Courtesy of Harold Bowtell*

Above: The Furness Railway railmotor at Lakeside, Windermere. *Courtesy of Bob Gregson*

Left: 'Cauliflower' No 28542 at Keswick station. *Courtesy of Bob Gregson*

Below: Ivatt 2-6-2 tank No 40011 at Boat of Garten in 1958, now part of the heritage Strathspey Railway.
Courtesy of Bob Gregson

were presenting long-forgotten musicals, revues and plays at various music halls throughout Britain:

Florodora company – Eccles to Preston
Miss Glossop Harrif's company – Birkenhead to Carlisle
The Master of the Mill company – Leeds to Manchester
When Knights Were Bold company – Bradford to Glasgow
A Royal Divorce company – Hyde to Glasgow
For Wife and Kingdom company – Barrow to Leith
The Slave Dealer company – Bolton to Cork
Miss Hook of Holland company – Blackpool to Dublin
The Arcadians company – Leeds to Manchester
Mr F. R. Benson's company – Liverpool to Birmingham
The Chocolate Soldier company – Oldham to Leeds
The Balkan Princess company – Secombe to Southport

The first of these was a rail journey from Eccles to Preston carrying the company that was bound for the Preston Empire for a performance of *Florodora*. At this veritable

Musicals of yesterday staged at the Preston Empire during the 1920s.
Courtesy of Pete Vickers

music hall, audiences enjoyed period musicals with staged performances of not only *Florodora*, *San Toy*, *The Arcadians* and *The Quaker Girl* well into the 1920s.

Railways came to be used not only by the promoters of pleasure but also as a foundation for cultural enjoyment. Paul Robeson, the great American bass singer, actor and activist, toured extensively in the late 1930s on the crack express, the 'Coronation Scot'.

Rails to Butlin's variety theatres

Notable entertainers, touring companies and travelling circus, actors, music hall performers, prima donnas and their audiences continued to place great reliance on the railways during the first half of the 20th century. The passengers also consisted of variety performers and audiences travelling to and from Butlin's holiday camps.

Billy Butlin offered West End stars the opportunity

Footplates and Footlights

Aboev: This famous streamlined train ceased to run with the outbreak of the Second World War.

Centre: 'Dinner is served, sir…' The menu contained interesting facts about the train, and Paul Robeson signed this copy for one lucky recipient.

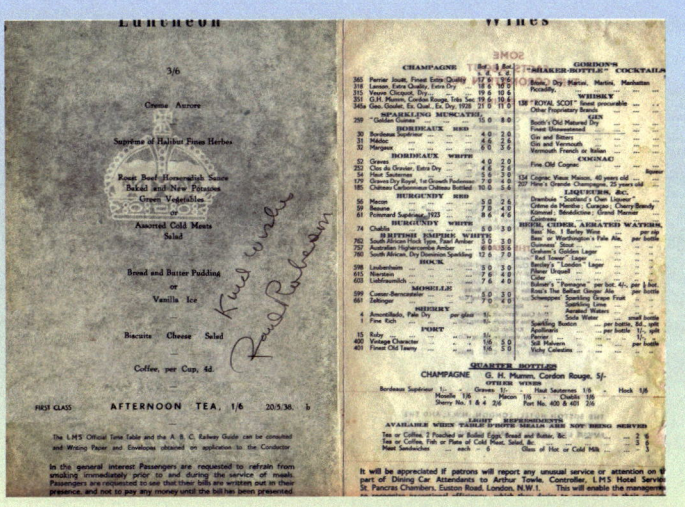

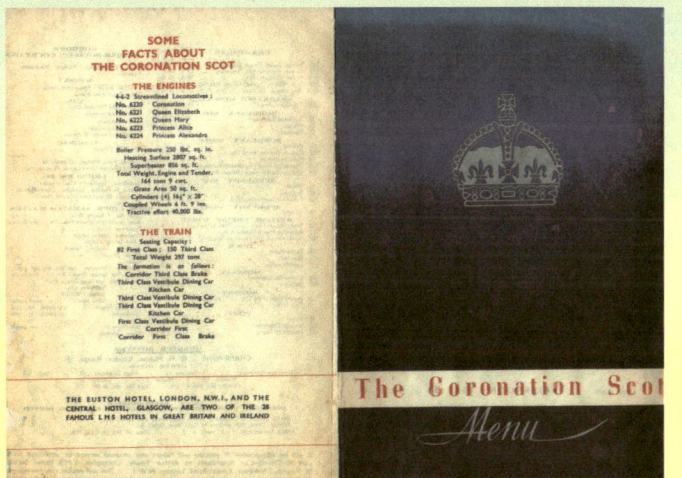

Above: Since Billy Butlin opened his first camp at Skegness in 1936, his holiday resort empire has become a social history in its own right. *Courtesy of Bob Gregson*

to perform on Sundays at Butlin's for a reduced fee on their day off from the London theatre. Moreover, it is surprising to know who they might have been entertaining out there in the audience. The first song that Paul McCartney sang in public was *Long Tall Sally* in a Butlin's talent contest. The group of Butlin's entertainers known as Redcoats has featured Cliff Richard, Des O'Connor, Michael Barrymore, Jimmy Tarbuck, Jimmy Cricket and Shane Ritchie, all of whom began their careers at Butlin's before becoming famous.

An LMS poster for Ayr, location of Butlin's Heads of Ayr camp. *Courtesy of Bob Gregson*

Above: Sir Billy Butlin is in good company in 1962 with Miss America and Miss Canada.

Below: 'B1' 4-6-0 No 61139 passes Peterborough with a 'Butlin's Express', carrying another bunch of holidaymakers bound for Filey holiday camp. *Courtesy of Bob Gregson*

Above: 'K1' Class No 62005 (now preserved) takes a breather at Filey after conveying a load of happy campers. *Courtesy of Bob Gregson*

Nine Butlin's camps throughout Britain were served by the railway network. The Filey camp had its own railway station, which opened in 1947 in the then East Riding of Yorkshire. The camp station was situated at the end of a short branch line off the line from Hull to Scarborough. It had four very long platforms to cater for the large numbers of holidaymakers arriving and departing from the holiday camp each Saturday during the holiday season, reminiscent of the television sitcom *Hi-de-hi!*, which was modelled on early days at Butlin's. However, passenger numbers dropped significantly as more people arrived at the camp by car, and the station closed to passengers on 17 July 1977.

Apart from the Filey branch serving Butlin's camp, the network of local branch lines and their appealing motive power were once pivotal to the rural landscape of England. Indeed, the tranquil railway scene saw minimal change and preserved the rustic essence and magnetism of the country's railway network for well over a century.

At about the time of the closure

Footplates and Footlights

'Coronation' Class No 6229 *Duchess of Hamilton* was retired to Butlin's Minehead. *Courtesy of Bob Gregson*

Trouble at the mill

In this section we look at concessions for music hall artists travelling by train the length and breadth of the country, and industrial disputes within the profession causing the formation of the Variety Artists Federation. There were financial advantages to music hall artists travelling by train if they had joined the Music Hall Artistes' Railway Association, which was set up in 1897 to secure cut-price fares from the railway companies. It soon had 5,000 members and was so successful that *The Stage* newspaper suggested that it should extend its scope to cover all aspects relating to music hall artists. The Association had been dissolved before 1916.

A Music Hall Artistes' Railway Association pass for 1933-34. *Author*

of the branch line from Kings Lynn to Hunstanton, the poet laureate John Betjeman appeared on a diesel multiple unit in a nostalgic film. Perhaps one of the most notable songs to be associated with railway closures was *The Slow Train*, with lyrics by Michael Flanders and music by Donald Swann.

The Furness Railway came to be used by those engaged in the music hall industry, with favourable terms offered for travelling music hall artists during 1897:

'On or after 1st October 1897 parties of music hall artists and their assistants, numbering five persons and upwards, will be conveyed distances above 20 miles at the undermentioned rate: single journey – three-fourths of the ordinary single fare, return journey – ordinary single fare and one half. The tickets to be made available until the end of the tour; ordinary paper tickets will be issued to stations endorsed, music hall artists, only one half the ordinary cloak room charges are to be made to music hall artists. Luggage will be a minimum of one penny per package.' (Furness Railway Audit Accounts Office, Barrow, 29 September 1897)

Thus music hall artists toured Britain and Ireland by train, often playing a different venue every day for months and with great reliance on theatre digs. But the average wage of music hall artists during the Edwardian period would be around £10 per week and, after paying for theatre digs and train fares, the less well-known performers probably felt destitute. Grievances became so heated among the music hall fraternity in the early years of the 20th century that on 18 February 1906 15 representatives of the Grand Order of Water Rats, the Beneficent Order of Terriers, the Music Hall Artistes Railway Association and the International Artist Lodge got together and decided to inaugurate the Variety Artistes Federation, a performers' union with the aim of protecting members' rights and achieving equitable agreement with management.

The development of the syndicates and their control over theatres increased tensions between employees and employers. Industrial disputes took place in London and peripheral halls in 1907, organised by the Variety Artistes Federation. The strikes ended in arbitration, which satisfied most of the main demands: a minimum wage and a maximum working week for musicians.

Further reading from David Hindle in the Silver Link Silk Editions series....

The focus of this book is the core route of the original Furness Railway from Carnforth to Barrow-in-Furness, Millom and Whitehaven. The line retains the title Furness Railway from Carnforth to Barrow-in-Furness and serves a number of Victorian resorts and small towns, principally Silverdale, Arnside, Grange-over-Sands, Ulverston and Dalton-in-Furness. North of Barrow-in-Furness the meandering and captivating route to Millom, Whitehaven, Workington and Carlisle is today aptly named the Cumbrian Coast Line.

Overall, *Enjoying the Cumbrian Coast Railway* is designed to appeal to lovers of the Lake District and its awesome countryside as well as tourists, railway historians and enthusiasts, photographers, hikers, cyclists, naturalists and in particular ornithologists.

Although there is a general acceptance by all that the wonderful days of steam have irrevocably gone, there is still a yearning for unashamed nostalgia. Accordingly a reawakening of memories is captured with a photographic portfolio of steam and diesel locomotives at work on the Furness Line throughout the book.

Chapter Two – The good old days?
Charles Dickens catches a train during *Hard Times*

The opening of Preston station and the arrival of the North Union Railway line from Wigan on 31 October 1838 saw the beginning of considerable railway development in the area, coinciding with the emergence of pub entertainment in singing saloons and the travelling circuses.

Charles Dickens travelled by train to Preston at the height of the Industrial Revolution to witness for himself the levels of economic and industrial strife during the terrible strike and lock-out of 1853-54 affecting the textile industry. During the severe winter of 1854 36 Preston firms locked out their workforce in a dispute over higher wages, and up to 20,000 were unemployed.

The town was described by Bradshaw in his Victorian railway guide as 'one of the principal manufacturing towns in the country. There are upwards of 50 cotton mills in the town.' Dickens captivatingly describes how he travelled from London Euston during February 1854 in his journalistic writings, 'Dickens – Miscellaneous Papers'.

Dickens puts on record:

'When I got to Preston, it was four o'clock in the afternoon. What I wanted to see with my own eyes was how these people acted under a mistaken impression, and what qualities they showed, even at that disadvantage, which ought to be the strength and peace – not the weakness and trouble – of the community.'

Dickens attended a meeting of delegates at the Old Cockpit and an

'Have a comfortable journey, sir.' Charles Dickens commenced his journey to Preston at Euston and would have passed under the Doric Arch, constructed in 1837. *Courtesy of Bob Gregson*

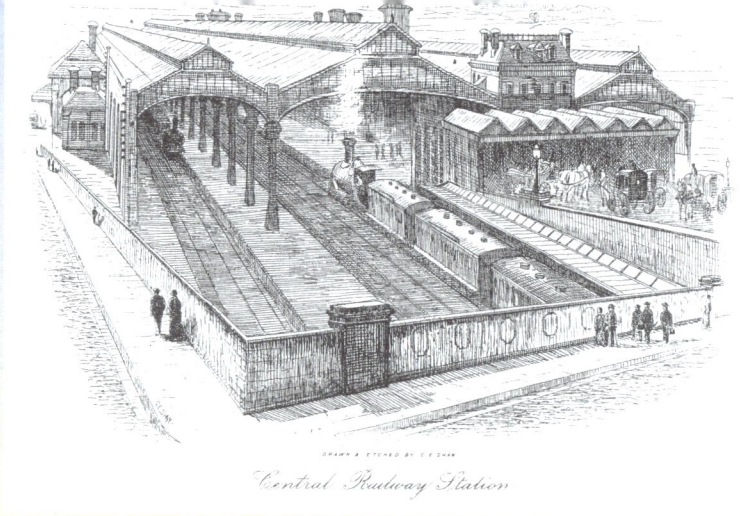

Charles Dickens arrived by train at the North Union Railway station at Preston in 1854. The station is depicted here by C. E. Shaw. *Author's collection*

Dickens may well have taken a Preston hansom cab and witnessed innumerable smoking chimneys and back-to-back terraced houses. *Courtesy of Bob Gregson*

open-air meeting held at The Orchard, where delegates pledged money to Preston operatives. Despite Dickens's honourable and altruistic intentions, he was soon to discover that Victorian Preston had no real claim to the adage 'the good old days of music hall'.

The good old days in Victorian Preston?
During his visit to Preston Dickens paints a clear picture of the social and economic scene there while staying at the Old Bull Hotel in Church Street. Significantly his experiences influenced his writing in the novel *Hard Times*, which is said to be based on Preston.

Judging by a February 1865 report in the *Preston Chronicle*, had Charles Dickens visited the local thief's kitchen he would probably encountered the Preston equivalent of Oliver Twist:

'Congregations of all sorts of men, women and children are gathered in the thief's kitchen. In all of them there are scales with which the proprietor weighs the bread begged by the tramps during the day, before he purchases it. In these places lads, women, men, girls, beggars, thieves, tramps, vagabonds, cripples and prostitutes sleep together, without any respect to age or any distinction of sex, huddling in imperfectly ventilated rooms, and taking off their clothing before retiring to rest on account of the vermin.'

There were 27 lodging houses of receivers of stolen goods, 31 public houses, 25 beer houses, two coffee shops, and six suspected houses, all of which were known resorts of thieves and prostitutes, and 61 brothels.

The first music halls were originally tavern rooms and singing saloons that provided entertainment for their patrons in the form of music and speciality acts. Dickens would have witnessed appalling conditions of depravity and decadence where hedonistic activities were doubtless sought in pub concert rooms, singing saloons and other dubious establishments. Nevertheless, the popular entertainment industry was a significant part of working-class culture and fundamentally it was in the singing saloons that music hall had its origin.

In 1865 a *Preston Chronicle* newspaper correspondent wrote:

'On a Saturday evening we set out with the intention of visiting a few of the cheap hops of which in Preston there are many… The second singing room we visited was up a flight of steps out of a stable yard, in a court not a hundred miles from the market place… Can any good emanate from such places…? Little by little the girl loses her modesty, and the end is as sure and certain as is the clergyman's hope of her joyful resurrection after her life of vice with its daily battling with hunger, and her wretched death in the workhouse infirmary.'

The prospect of incarceration in the one of the town's parish workhouses or in the single union workhouse first established in 1868 was a daunting one. In the above passage the girl's 'wretched death in the workhouse infirmary' epitomises tragic stories of sadness and misfortune that are sometimes told about workhouse inmates.

The first Preston concert room audiences integrated young working-class factory workers, but were not gender specific, and were they affordable? At the time of the 1851 Preston census the small professional and clerical sector earned the highest wages. About half the population were engaged in artisan occupations and skilled workers could earn more than 20 shillings per week during good times, but many were less regularly employed. For those women who did not work in factories, the largest single occupation was domestic service. There were tradesmen and shopkeepers of all kinds, together with the proprietors of beer houses and public houses scattered around the town. Perhaps the poorest of all were the charwomen and itinerant salesmen, many of whom were almost totally destitute.[16]

'By the mid-19th century factory work was the basis of Preston's prosperity, with around 25,000 people employed by 64 textile firms during 1850.'[17] The textile industry helped create a new urban industrialised sixfold increase in the population of Preston during the first half of the 19th century. Despite the severe economic hardship that resulted from the peak of the cotton famine circa 1863, the working classes sustained their interest in the commercial pub music hall industry in the town, which varied in tone from the purpose-built and reputable King's Head and George music halls to the grossly licentious singing saloons. The above scenes were hardly consistent with the parable of the good old days of the mid-1860s.

Charles Dickens would have witnessed abject poverty, appalling housing conditions, disease and high infant mortality – emphatically not a music hall joke during the so-called good old days. The strike and lock-out of 1854 lasted for 39 weeks, and after the longest cotton mill strike there was the great cotton famine of 1861.

Dickens again visited Preston in April 1867 and gave readings from *A Christmas Carol* and *The Pickwick Papers* to a packed audience at the town's Theatre Royal, with Dress Circle seats costing 4 shillings, before departing for another Lancashire cotton town, Blackburn.

Chapter Three – Accolade: Maybe it's because I'm a Londoner

Dickens on London's first Victorian music halls

'The music hall, as it is at present understood, was started many years ago at the Canterbury Hall over the water. The entertainments proving popular, the example was speedily followed in every quarter of the town. The performance in no way differs, except in magnitude, from those which are to be seen in every town of any importance throughout the country. Ballet, gymnastics, and so-called comic-singing, form the staple of the bill of fare, but nothing comes foreign to the music hall proprietor. Performing animals, winners of walking matches, successful scullers, shipwrecked sailors, swimmers of the channel, conjurers, ventriloquists, tight-rope dancers, campanologists, clog-dancers, sword-swallowers, velocipedists, champion skaters, imitators, marionettes, decanter equilibrists, champion shots, living models of marble gems, statue marvels, fire princes, mysterious youths, spiral bicycle ascensionists, flying children, empresses of the air, kings of the wire, vital sparks, Mexican boneless wonders, white-eyed musical Kaffirs, strong-jawed ladies, cannon-ball performers, illuminated fountains, and that remarkable musical eccentricity the orchestre militaire, all have had their turn on the music hall stage.

'Strangers to the business may be warned that the word turn, as understood in the profession, means the performance for which the artist is engaged, and frequently comprises four or more songs, however, much or little of pleasure the first effort may have given the audience. Furthermore, as many of the popular performers take several turns nightly, it is undesirable to visit many of these establishments on the same evening, as it is quite possible to go to four or five halls in different parts of the town, and to find widely diverse stages occupied by the same sets of performers. Among the principal halls may be mentioned the Bedford, in Camden Town; the Canterbury, Westminster-bridge Road; the Foresters, Cambridge Road; Gattis, Westminster-bridge road; the London Pavilion, at the top of the Haymarket; Evans, Covent-garden; the Metropolitan, Edgware-road; the Oxford, Oxford Street; the Cambridge, 136, Commercial Street; Lusby's Palace, Mile End Road; and Wilton's in Well Close Square, in the far east. Of these the Canterbury, the Metropolitan, and the South London have a speciality for ballet on a large scale. The Canterbury has an arrangement for ventilation peculiar to itself. A large portion of the roof is so arranged as to admit of its easy and rapid removal and replacement.

'The entertainments at the other halls vary only in degree. The operatic selections, which were at one time the distinguishing feature of the Oxford, have of late years been discontinued. A curiosity in the way of music halls may be found by the explorer at the Bell, in St George Street, Ratcliff-highway, where, contrary to precedent, the Negro element preponderates among the audience instead of on the stage. The hours of performance at most music halls are from about 8pm till 11.30pm, and the prices of admission vary from 6d to 3s. Private boxes, at varying prices, may be had at nearly all the music-halls.'

In the above taken from *Dickens's Dictionary of London* of 1879, edited by his son, also Charles, Dickens alludes to several music halls including the Canterbury and Wilton's, which were two of the capital's earliest. Charles Morton purchased the old Canterbury Arms, Lambeth, in December 1849, and presented concert performances on three nights a week. In 1852 Morton opened an adjacent concert hall, markedly separate from the public house. He presented ballet and opera in concert form, as well as variety, and is known to have presented the first performance of Gounod's *Faust*, sung in English. Morton's Canterbury Hall was a key building in the history of music hall and the architectural forerunner of a whole new generation of buildings. The hall was further extended, although it was not, as is often said, the very first music hall. Canterbury Hall was later rebuilt as a variety theatre and finally destroyed by bombing in 1942.

Another early music hall was The Middlesex, Drury Lane (1851). Popularly known as the 'Old Mo', it was built on the site of the Mogul Saloon. Later converted into a theatre, it was demolished in 1965, and the New London Theatre stands on its site. The Oxford Music Hall (1861) in Oxford Street was built by Charles Morton on the site of an old coaching inn called the Boar & Castle.

The Eagle was an East End tavern on the corner of City Road and Shepherdess Walk, London, and presented regular musical entertainment. The nursery rhyme 'Pop goes the Weasel' features the Eagle, and tells the story of a father spending his weekly wage in the music halls and then, to raise additional money, having to 'pop' or pawn his 'weasel', which is thought to refer to a piece of equipment in the tailoring industry. Tailoring was one of the main occupations in London's East End. The Eagle did a roaring trade as one of the first music halls. Marie Lloyd, who would become one of the biggest music hall stars of all, appeared there in 1885, at the age of 14.

Charles Dickens was a regular visitor and wrote about the experience in *Sketches by Boz*. The Eagle was sold in 1883 to the Salvation Army, perennial enemy of drink and the music halls. The

The Canterbury Hall music hall, London, in 1908.
Courtesy of Bob Gregson

building has since been demolished and the site now boasts a new Eagle pub, which has a display of old music hall prints.

The nature and appeal of the early Victorian pub/music hall reached its zenith in around the 1860s and '70s. By 1865 there were 32 music halls in London, seating between 500 and 5,000 people, together with an unknown, but larger, number of smaller venues. Numbers peaked in 1878, with 78 music halls in the capital and 300 minor halls. Legislation detailed in Chapter One demonstrates their ultimate demise.

The variety theatres of London

By the late Victorian era the level of congeniality inherited from the singing saloon had been transposed to the new variety theatres, and police were in attendance to uphold the high standards of the manager. The halls created a demand for new and catchy popular songs, and as a result professional songwriters were enlisted to provide the music for a range of star performers including, most notably, Marie Lloyd, Dan Leno, Little Tich and George Leybourne.

Music halls and variety theatres also featured an annual Christmas pantomime. To this day pantomime fuels the imagination at Christmas with fairy stories about Cinderella, Aladdin, Jack and the Beanstalk and many more to delight families with shouts of 'He's behind you!' 'Oh yes he is,' or conversely 'Oh no he's not.' Or perhaps he's just well hidden! London and every provincial town and city had its own enchanting pantomime as necessary as sparkling Christmas cards.

Dan Leno. *Courtesy of Bob Gregson*

A London Pavilion programme for a production featuring Douglas Fairbanks in Robin Hood. *Author's collection*

Accolade: Maybe it's because I'm a Londoner

A new era of variety theatre was introduced with the rebuilding of the London Pavilion in 1885. The level of refinement changed the image of music halls, which began to resemble the established legitimate theatre. With their classical façades, the purpose-built variety theatres were adorned with architectural splendour, baroque auditoria and elegant foyers.

One of the most famous of London's West End music halls was the Empire, Leicester Square. The Empire Theatre opened on 17 April 1884 as a West End variety theatre, as well as a ballet venue, with a capacity of about 2,000.

In 1887 the theatre reopened as a popular music hall named the Empire Theatre of Varieties. In March 1896 it played host to the first commercial theatrical performances of a projected film to a UK audience by Auguste and Louis Lumière; the film programme ran for 18 months. Over the next few years the theatre began to offer

The Gaiety Theatre, located in Aldwych, London, started life as a music hall in 1903, but was demolished in 1956. *Author's collection*

Above: A scene long gone: the Alhambra Music Hall, Leicester Square, illustrated in a programme dated 17 January 1898. *Courtesy of Bob Gregson*

a programme of live performances with short film shows known in the trade as cine-variety. Long gone as a live theatre, the rebuilt Empire is now a multi-screen cinema.

The Alhambra in Leicester Square was

built in 1860, in the former premises of the London Panopticon. This sophisticated venue was noted for its alluring corps de ballet and was a focal point for West End pleasure-seekers. It was demolished in 1936.

Theatrical entrepreneur Richard D'Oyly Carte opened his Royal English Opera House in 1891 on Shaftesbury Avenue. During 1892, D'Oyly Carte sold the theatre to a company headed by Sir Augustus Harris of the Theatre Royal, and it became a newly established music hall known as the Palace of Varieties, which opened on 10 December 1892. In 1893 Charles Morton became Managing Director; a man of vast experience, he had founded the Canterbury Hall music hall. Famous music hall stars graced the Palace stage for more than 20 years, including Vesta Tilley, George Robey, Marie Lloyd, Little Tich, Vesta Victoria, John Tilley's Palace Girls, and many more.

The theatre staged early adult entertainment by featuring apparently nude women, although the girls who featured in these displays were actually wearing flesh-toned body stockings and were not naked at all.

In more modern times the poet laureate Sir John Betjeman added his own tribute

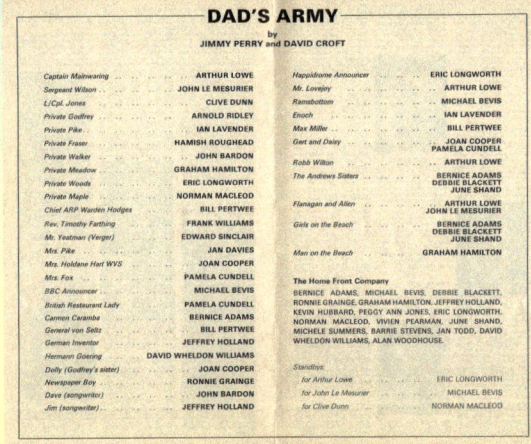

Left: A rare colour photo of a show at the Alhambra. *Courtesy of Bob Gregson*

Above: 'Right, pay attention and don't panic!' The immortal cast of Dad's Army on stage at the Shaftesbury Theatre in October 1975. *Author's collection*

when he described the architecture of the historic Palace Theatre:
'In London, the noblest surviving building – in my opinion more impressive within and without than Covent Garden – is the Royal English Opera House (1891, Thomas Calcutt architect), now called the Palace Theatre… The Palace is the only theatre architecture in London, or for that matter in the provinces of the last 60 years, which climbs into the regions as a work of art.'

Like so many former music halls and variety theatres today, the Palace is now

Vesta Tilley starred at the Palace Theatre, Shaftsbury Avenue, London. *Courtesy of Bob Gregson*

Above and right: Between 1893 and 1904 Charles Morton managed the Palace Theatre. It became one of the foremost variety theatres in London. *Author's collection*

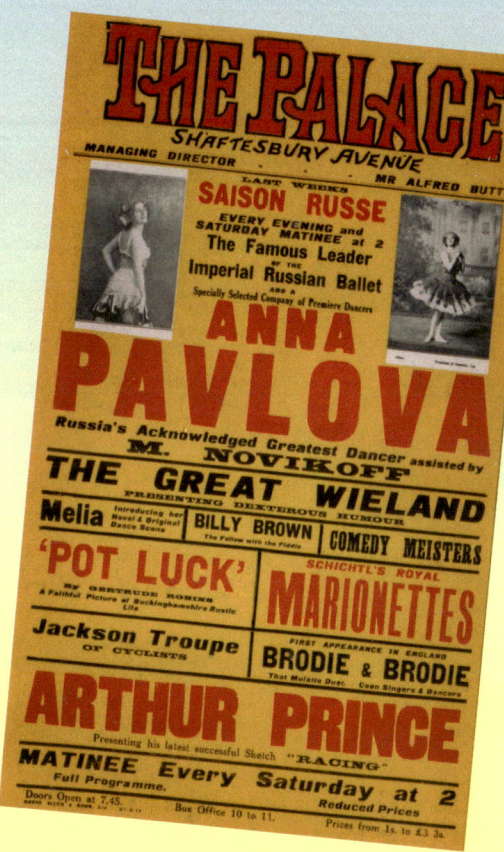

the home of long-running musicals. It is possible to observe the entire unusual and fine-looking red-brick theatre from Charing Cross Road; stop to admire the Spanish Renaissance-style exterior.

King Edward VII died on 6 May 1910, and though not the end of music hall, his reign will always be associated with the names of some of its greatest stars. The acceptance of the music hall genre as a legitimate cultural form was established by the first Royal Variety Performance in the presence of King George V during 1912 at London's Palace Theatre. Consistent with this new respectability in music hall, Marie Lloyd was excluded from the performance, despite her fame, probably because her songs exploited sexual naughtiness and innuendo, and captured and shocked her audience from the start.

The Metropolitan was a West End music hall in Edgware Road and one of the last of the genre to be demolished in London. The original building on this site, the White Lion Inn, dated from 1524. In 1836 this was rebuilt to become 'Turnham's Grand Concert Hall'. Then in 1862 rebuilding commenced, at a cost of £25,000, ending in 1864 with an increased capacity of 2,000, and a new name, 'The Metropolitan Music Hall'. 'The Great Vance' made his London debut there in 1864, complete

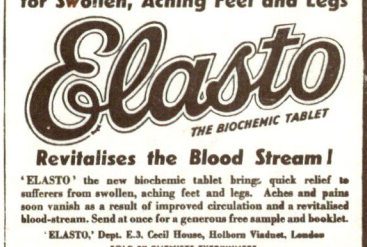

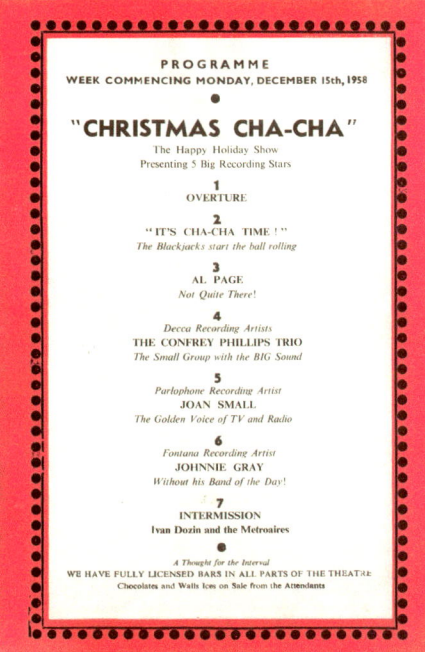

Above: Commencing on Monday 15 December, 1958, the London Metropolitan Music Hall presented Christmas Cha-Cha (complete with pereiod ads). *Author's collection*

Left: The Winter Garden Theatre played its final production, Alice In Wonderland, in January 1960. Following demolition, the New London Theatre was built on the site in 1973.

with monocle and evening dress, portraying the period swell. Notwithstanding contemporary performers like Vance, the theatre was redesigned in 1896 by Frank Matcham with a new and enlarged stage, new dressing rooms and a new auditorium seating 1,855. It reopened once more in 1897 as The Metropolitan Theatre and continued as a London music hall. However, with the decline in popularity of music hall many theatres were abandoned or converted to other uses, especially as cinemas, and their interiors were lost. Sadly, the Metropolitan was one such example; its last role was that of a television studio, until final closure and demolition in 1964.

Fortunately many fine and historic theatres in London survive, several of which began as music halls: the Hackney Empire, Victoria Palace, London Palladium and Coliseum are all examples that are described in subsequent chapters.

One of the finest and oldest working theatres in London is the amazing Theatre Royal, Drury Lane. I often pause in Covent Garden to marvel at its Regency façade and fascinating history. The theatre building is the most recent in a line of four theatres that were built at the same location, the earliest of which dated back to 1663, making it the oldest theatre site in London still in use. Although never, in broad terms, a generic music hall, I nevertheless cite this theatre as an example of a great London theatre.

The Theatre Royal, Drury Lane, London
The Theatre Royal, commonly known as Drury Lane, is a Grade I listed building in Covent Garden. The present theatre is owned by the composer Andrew Lloyd Webber.

The first theatre on the site was built at the behest of Thomas Killigrew, when theatres were allowed to reopen during the English Restoration. The new playhouse, architect unknown, opened on 7 May 1663

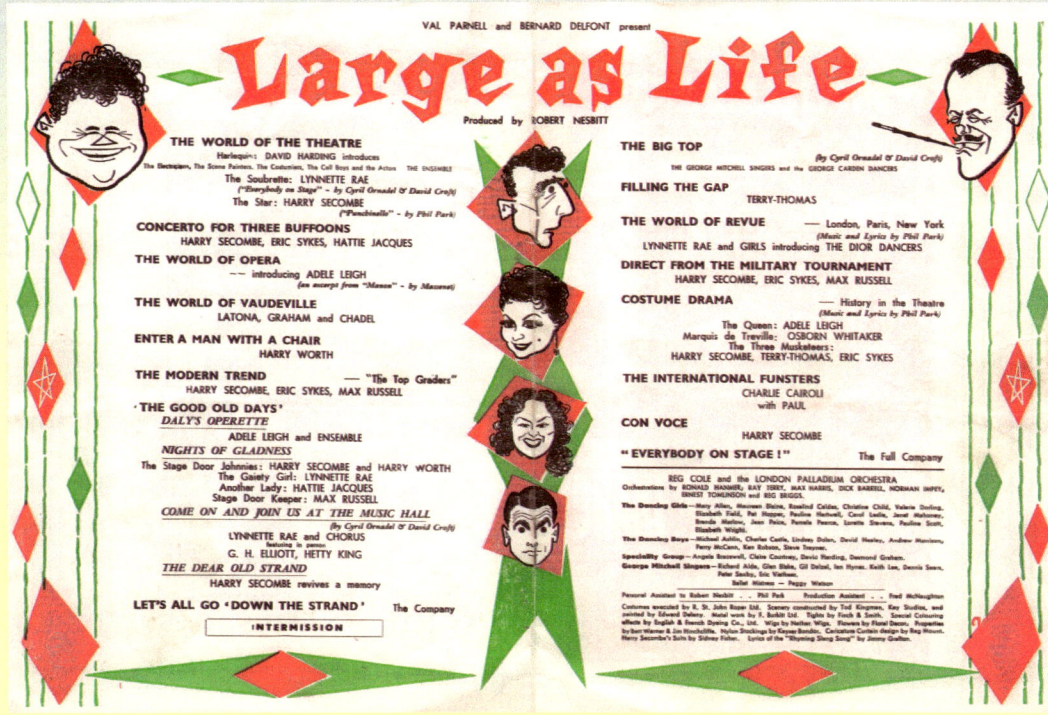

This London Palladium revue starred Harry Secombe, Terry-Thomas and a 'Concerto for Three Buffoons'! Author's collection

and was known from the location of its entrance as the Theatre Royal in Bridges Street. For its first two centuries it was one of a handful of patent theatres, granted monopoly rights to the production of legitimate drama in London.

The King himself frequently attended the theatre's productions, as did Samuel Pepys, whose private diaries provide much of what we know of London theatre-going in the 1660s. Located well to the west of the City boundary, the theatre was unaffected by the Great Fire of London, which raged through the City in September 1666, but it burned down six years later on 25 January 1672.

Killigrew built a larger theatre on the same plot, opening in 1674. Joseph Grimaldi is best known for his development of the modern-day white-face clown and popularised this in many pantomimes, making his stage debut in 1780. The theatre was in need of updating by the end of the 18th century and was demolished in 1791. This building had lasted nearly 120 years. In 1791, under Richard Brinsley Sheridan's management, the building was demolished again to make way for a larger theatre, which was opened on 12 March 1794.

The new Drury Lane was a cavernous theatre, accommodating more than 3,600 spectators, but it was to survive for only 15 years. An assassination attempt on King George III took place at the theatre on 15 May 1800, then on 24 February 1809 it burned down; on being encountered drinking a glass of wine in the street while watching the fire, Sheridan was famously reported to have said, 'A man may surely be allowed to take a glass of wine by his own fireside.'

The present Theatre Royal, designed by Benjamin Dean Wyatt, opened on 10 October 1812 with a production of *Hamlet*. It made some concessions toward intimacy, seating 3,060 people, about 550 fewer than the previous building (though it is still

The Theatre Royal, Drury Lane. *Courtesy of LW Theatres*

considered an extremely large theatre).

On 6 September 1817 it became the first British theatre to be lit by gas throughout. In 1820 the portico that still stands at the theatre's front entrance on Catherine Street was added. The colonnade running down the Russell Street side of the building was added in 1831.

Productions relying on spectacle became the norm at Drury Lane. The 1909 play, *The Whip*, featured not only a working locomotive and train crash but also a chamber of horrors and 12 horses recreating the 2,000 Guinea stakes on an on-stage treadmill.

The last major interior renovation was in 1922, under the ownership of managing director Sir Alfred Butt, at a cost of £150,000, leaving a four-tiered theatre able to seat just over 2,000 people. Composer and performer Ivor Novello, immensely popular in his time, presented his musicals in Drury Lane from 1931 until the theatre was closed in 1939 at the outbreak of the Second World War.

In the post-war years, the theatre staged Rodgers & Hammerstein's new musicals: *Oklahoma!*, *Carousel*, *South Pacific* and *The King and I*. Many more musicals have made their debut at Drury Lane and continue to do so to this day. The building was Grade I listed in February 1958.

Author Tom Ogden calls the Theatre Royal as one of the world's most haunted theatres. The 'man in grey' is said to appear in the upper circle, dressed as a nobleman of the late 18th century. Legend says that he is the ghost of a knife-stabbed man whose skeletal remains were found within a walled-up side passage in 1848. Joseph Grimaldi is reported to be a helpful apparition, purportedly guiding nervous actors skilfully about the stage on more than one occasion.

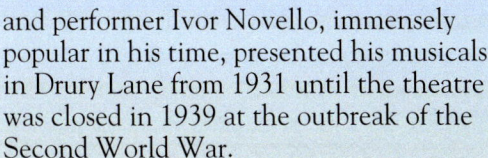

The Theatre Royal Drury Lane.
Courtesy of LW Theatres

Chapter Four – Frank Matcham: Theatre architect extraordinaire

Frank Matcham.

Frank Matcham was born in Devon, the son of a brewery clerk, on 22 November 1854. In 1868 he became apprenticed to George Bridgman, a local builder and architect. In the mid-1870s he moved to London to join the architectural practice of Jethro Robinson, who was consulting theatre architect to the Lord Chamberlain.

In 1877 Matcham married Robinson's daughter. The following year, when Robinson died suddenly, the 24-year-old took over the practice. He formed his own practice, Matcham & Co, in the 1880s and enlisted skilled craftsman whom he used on all of his projects. In his spare time he visited many of London's buildings, of varying ages, but took a particular liking to theatres and music halls.

A building of special interest to Frank Matcham was the newly completed Gaiety Theatre in the Strand, designed by Charles Phipps. Matcham was impressed by how Phipps utilised a small, awkward plot but still managed to build a theatre of normal size. He probably gained inspiration from the Gaiety, as some of his later theatres were built on restricted plots of land. Matcham went from success to success and over the next 30 years became unrivalled as the most prolific theatre architect of all time.

Frank Matcham designed at least 80 theatres as original architect and was involved in minor and major rebuilds of 80 more between 1873 and 1913. According to the dramatist Alan Bennett, there was a Matcham theatre in every corner of the UK.

Matcham's most successful period was between 1892 and 1912 when he worked extensively for Moss Empires, the theatrical company headed by Edward Moss and run by Oswald Stoll. He completed 21 theatres for Moss and Stoll, most of which were variety theatres in the provinces. Matcham retired to Southend-on-Sea, Essex, before the First World War, where he died of a heart attack on 17 May 1920.

Today it is thought that five-sixths of Matcham's work has been destroyed, especially during the mid-20th century with the demise of the Moss Empire variety theatres, though what remain are national icons. A total of 28 buildings are now protected by statute, including the Leeds County Arcade, Harrogate Royal Hall and the Blackpool Tower Ballroom of 1899, as well as notable theatres in London and the provinces. Surviving London theatres include the London Hippodrome (1900), restored but now a gaming casino, Hackney Empire (1901), Coliseum (1904), Palladium (1910), Victoria Palace (1911), Lyric

Frank Matcham: Theatre architect extraordinaire

Theatre, Hammersmith, and Richmond Theatre (1899).

Surviving provincial Matcham theatres include the Kings, Southsea; New Theatre Royal, Portsmouth; Bristol Hippodrome; Grand Opera House, Belfast; Royal Hall, Harrogate; Buxton Opera House; Olympia, Liverpool; Theatre Royal, Newcastle; Empire Edinburgh; Kings, Glasgow; His Majesty's, Aberdeen; Grand Theatre, Blackpool; and the Gaiety Theatre, Isle of Man.

The Ardwick Empire, latterly known as the Ardwick Green Hippodrome, opened its doors on 18 July 1904, and enjoyed success with live theatre before showing some films from 1930. It was updated in 1935 and re-branded the New Manchester Hippodrome,

Right: Everyone a masterpiece: Matcham's Buxton Opera House.

Above: The splendid auditorium of the Gaiety Theatre, Isle of Man. *Courtesy of Richard Slee, 'Visit Isle of Man'*

Above: Sadly, now just a memory: the old Ardwick Green Hippodrome. *Courtesy of Bob Gregson*

continuing until it closed on 22 April 1961; left empty, it was damaged by fire in 1964 and demolished.

Surviving Frank Matcham theatres

The Kursaal – Harrogate's Royal Hall:
Though not a music hall building or theatre in the true sense of the word, Harrogate's Royal Hall staged generic music hall and variety acts. It is a unique entertainment complex and is accredited Grade II* listing, as a well-preserved example of the work of Frank Matcham.

The development of Harrogate as a spa town by the mid-19th century saw the building of a number of facilities associated with both taking the waters and the

On 21 December, 1956 Tommy Cooper starred in the panto *Puss in Boots* at the Ardwick Green Hippodrome. *Author's collection*

The Manchester Hippodrome opened on Boxing Day 1904 in Oxford Street, Manchester. It had only a short lifespan before being closed in March 1935 and demolished to make way for the Gaumont Theatre on the same site. *Courtesy of Bob Gregson*

production of various entertainments. The idea of a kursaal came from the continent, where such complexes were normal centrepieces in spa towns, though rare in England; the first building of this kind was probably a hotel in Baden Baden in 1809.

A kursaal is essentially a grand reception hall and place of occasion for a spa town. However, a competition to design such a building for the spa town of Harrogate was held in 1899 and was won by Robert Beale. The building was attached to the pre-existing Concert Room of 1835 and opened with a concert conducted by Sir Hubert Parry on 27 May 1903.

The German word 'kursaal' became incompatible with a surge of patriotism at the time of the outbreak of the First World War in 1914. Consequently the name was changed to the Coliseum in 1915, and by Royal decree it became the Royal Hall in 1918. Nevertheless, the original name Kursaal is still prominently engraved on the stone façade of the building. The eventual design was heavily modified and the interior completely designed by Frank Matcham, who in practice became the senior consultant architect on the scheme, with Beale having responsibility for the structure. Matcham's genius with fibrous plaster gave the Kursaal its breathtaking interior. His use of fabric and furnishings enriched with extravagant decorative rendering of gold leaf was truly awesome.

The leading theatrical journal of the time, *The Era*, reported on Matcham's architecture on the 30 May 1903, describing his undoubted skill and expertise:

'This magnificent hall may be described as a palace of gold, glittering in light, softened by an abundance of cream tints into a harmonising effect, whilst up in the dome is a patch of blue, gleaming with stars of gold, relieving the architecture which throughout is rich in design.

Marble is freely used in the base of the hall

The Royal Hall, Harrogate. *Courtesy of Mike Hine*

A fish-eye lens view of the magnificent auditorium. *Courtesy of Royal Hall, Harrogate*

and round grey pillars of this material rise from the boxes to support the balcony. The boxes themselves are upholstered in pink, whilst the glamour of gold and cream is relieved by the opal cups, which form the electric light pendants. At the rear of the grand circle is another spacious promenade which is richly treated with Lincrusta work and enriched with figure subjects. Various portions of the ceiling are enriched with tapestry work.'

The Royal Hall presented a lexicon of entertainment and music hall entertainers at a time when Harrogate was served by the North Eastern Railway. Marie Lloyd trod the boards here on 17 June 1916, and other music hall and variety artists over the years included Lillie Langtry, Hetty King, Vesta Tilley, Harry Lauder, Dan Leno, Will Fyffe, Stanley Holloway, Gracie Fields, Robb Wilton, Frankie Howard, Louis Armstrong, The Beverley Sisters, Norman Wisdom, Ken Dodd and Sir Cliff Richard.

For well over a century the Royal Hall has presented an eclectic range of entertainment with programmes featuring dance bands, music hall, ballet and opera, drama, cinema, and orchestral concerts. Notably, the first performance of Sir Edward Elgar's 2nd Symphony was performed here on 9 August 1911, and the legendary

The view from the stage of the Royal Hall. *Courtesy of Royal Hall, Harrogate*

From Sir Edward Elgar *(left)* to Cliff Richard *(right)* and the Beatles – they have all performed at the Royal Hall, Harrogate. *Courtesy of Royal Hall, Harrogate*

Far right: A plan of Blackpool Grand Theatre at time of opening, with laudable comments from distinguished actors of the time. *Author*

Frank Matcham: Theatre architect extraordinaire

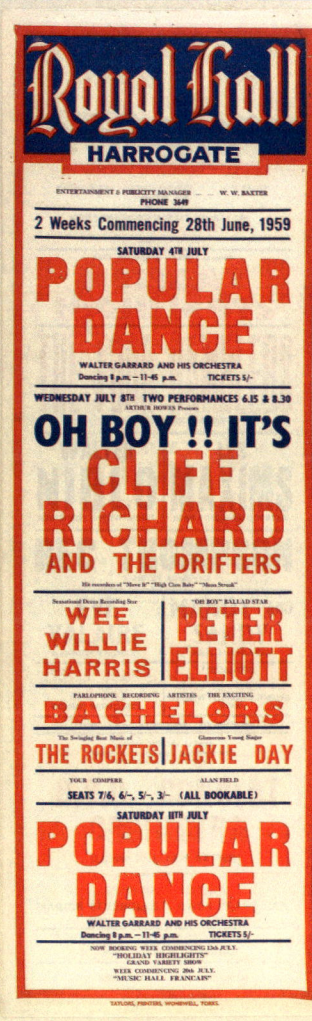

composer conducted his own Violin Concerto on 22 September 1927. The Beatles toured Britain in the early 1960s and the Harrogate Royal Hall was on their itinerary on 8 March 1963.

Blackpool Grand Theatre: Built at a cost of £20,000 on the site of a circus, the manager, Thomas Sergenson, opened the Blackpool Grand Theatre in 1894 with a performance of *Hamlet* starring Wilson Barrett. He had engaged the architect Frank Matcham to design the theatre and it had taken nine months to build. Sergenson drew leading performers of the day Lillie Langtry, Beerbohm Tree and Seymour Hicks. In 1909 he sold out to the Blackpool Tower Company for £47,500.

Today Frank Matcham's Blackpool masterwork survives to embody the glories of the late-Victorian theatre. The importance of Matcham's work does not only lie in the exquisite surface appearance but also in the way he pioneered technical innovation in theatre construction.

Before the 1890s theatre balconies had been supported by columns that obstructed sightlines. For the first time Matcham's pioneering use of long-span steel beams and cantilevers transformed theatre design and allowed the three tiers of the Grand to be built out into the auditorium without

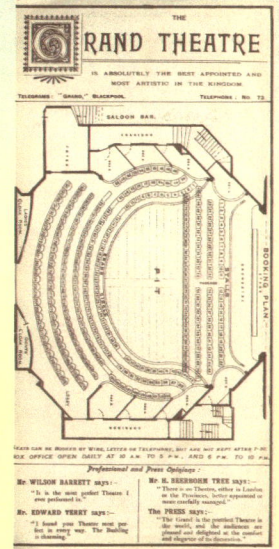

the use of supporting pillars.

This Victorian treasure was built as the prettiest theatre in the kingdom, but it was only to be spared the bulldozers in the nick of time in the early 1970s. In 1968 the theatre was sold to EMI and four years later, in 1972, it closed. It was initially saved from demolition by Grade II* listing in 1971, and by the venerable campaigner Major A. Burt Briggs of Lytham St Annes, who helped spearhead a successful campaign following closure. I was privileged to interview Burt Briggs at his home in 1998, when he informed me that he was the grandson of William Henry Broadhead, of the Lancashire-based theatre and show business entrepreneurial family. He informed me that the theatre had never been a music hall, although it attracted many great 20th-century actors, including Alec Guinness, Anna Neagle, James Mason and Noel Coward, and many more have trod the boards of the Blackpool Grand.

The Grand was briefly a bingo hall in the 1970s, then was taken over by the Friends of The Grand and reopened by the Grand Theatre Trust on 23 March 1981 with a performance of *The Merchant of Venice* starring Prunella Scales and Timothy West. Fotunately Matcham's masterpiece survives as a working theatre.

Lancaster Grand Theatre
Another Lancashire theatre, the Grand Theatre, Lancaster, is one of the oldest surviving theatres in England, opening in 1782. In 1897 Frank Matcham designed and supervised an extensive re-modelling of the stage and auditorium but a major fire in 1908 gutted the interior of the Grand, virtually destroying Matcham's work. Less than eight months later, it reopened in an Edwardian design which the theatre retains to the present day.

The London Palladium is a 2,286-seat Grade II* theatre located in Argyll Street in the City of Westminster. From the roster of stars that have played here and many televised performances, it is arguably the most famous theatre in London and the United Kingdom, especially for musical variety shows.

Walter Gibbons built the Palladium in 1910 as a premier

The renowned London Palladium. *Courtesy of LW Theatres*

variety theatre, to compete with Sir Edward Moss's London Hippodrome and Sir Oswald Stoll's London Coliseum. The theatre was rebuilt a year later by Fredrick Hengler, the son of a tightrope walker, as a circus arena for entertainments that embraced promenade concerts, pantomimes and an aquatic display in a flooded ring. However, the ring failed and the Palladium was redesigned by Frank Matcham as yet another masterpiece by the great theatre architect. It retains many of its original features, and had its own telephone system so that the occupants of boxes could call one another. However, the famous (but outdated) revolving stage has been removed to make way for more modern technology.

In 1928 the Palladium staged cine-variety for three months, but then became dark for a short period later in the same year and was close to bankruptcy. However, on 3 September of that year it reopened under the directorship of the impresario George Black, as part of the General Theatre Corporation (GTC). He revived its fortunes by returning to the staging of variety shows with both Britain's top home-grown acts and big American stars for two-week engagements.

Under Black's management the Palladium gained the reputation of 'The World's Leading Variety Theatre'. In 1935

The two Royal Variety Performances illustrated here were in the presence of His Majesty King George VI and Queen Elizabeth in 1950, and Queen Elizabeth II in 1952. Both shows featured famous music hall acts of yesteryear. *Author's collection*

Black initiated the Crazy Gang revues, which continued as an annual event at the Palladium until they transferred to the Victoria Palace Theatre in 1940. Black managed the Palladium until his death in 1945, then Val Parnell took over as Managing Director. He adopted a successful policy of presenting high-priced, big-name American acts at the top of the bill, including for example Judy Garland,

Sophie Tucker, Danny Kaye, Bing Crosby, Bob Hope, Liza Minnelli, Lena Horne, Ella Fitzgerald, Frank Sinatra and Sammy Davis Junior. Meanwhile many British stars of the day were relegated to second-billing.

The theatre has hosted the Royal Variety Performance a record 41 times, most recently in 2017.

From 1955 to 1967 the theatre was the setting for the top-rated ITV variety show *Sunday Night at the London Palladium*, hosted first by Tommy Trinder, followed by Bruce Forsyth, Norman Vaughan and Jimmy Tarbuck.

In 1961 it was announced that there would be no more straightforward variety bills at the Palladium, and Val Parnell began to sell theatres for redevelopment. In 1966 this fate awaited the London Palladium, the Victoria Palace and the Theatre Royal, Drury Lane. Fortunately, Prince Littler organised a take-over to save the theatres, and Val Parnell retired to live in France. With the demise of variety acts, the Palladium's stage has seen many musicals in the 21st century and still plays host to top performing celebrities.

The Beatles played the Palladium on 13th October 1963. In 1970 the theatre attempted to get Elvis Presley to perform 14 shows over a period of seven days. When Presley's manager, Tom Parker, heard that the theatre was offering Elvis Presley $28,000, he reportedly said, 'That's fine for me, now how much can you get for Elvis?' Presley never performed outside North America due to Parker's lack of a passport.

In 2000 ownership of the theatre changed once again when Stoll Moss was acquired by Andrew Lloyd Webber's Really Useful Theatre Group. While the theatre has a resident show, it is still able to have one-off performances; this is enabled by the scenery of the resident show being designed to be easily removed.

In 2018 Bruce Forsyth's ashes were laid to rest under the Palladium's stage, with a blue plaque commemorating him on a nearby wall, inscribed: 'Without question the UK's greatest entertainer, he rests in peace within the sound of music, laughter and dancing; exactly where he would want to be.'

Victoria Palace Theatre began life as a small concert room above the stables of the Royal Standard Hotel, a small hotel and tavern built in 1832 on the site of the present theatre. The hotel was demolished in 1886, by which time the Victoria railway terminus had opened. The railway companies were at this time building grand hotel structures at their termini, and the new Grosvenor Hotel at Victoria was one of

The Victoria Palace Theatre once hosted traditional variety, such as the famous Crazy Gang during 1959. *Author's collection*

the first. Added to this was the integration of the electric underground system. Like many of London's major transport hubs, Victoria station was very convenient for the music halls and theatres of London's West End.

The concert room became the Royal Standard music hall, but it was demolished in 1910 and replaced, at a cost of £12,000, by the Victoria Palace Theatre; again designed by prolific theatre architect Frank Matcham, it opened on 6 November 1911.

The Victoria Palace Theatre continued the music hall tradition by presenting mainly variety. From 1947 Jack Hylton produced the Crazy Gang series of comedy revues, with a glittering company of variety performers including Flanagan and Allen, Nervo and Knox, and Naughton and Gold. The long-running Black and White Minstrel Show played through the 1960s until 1972. Another unusually long-running show at the theatre was *Buddy – The Buddy Holly Story*, which played for 13 years in London from 1989. After this the theatre presented mostly revivals of well-known musicals.

In 2014 the theatre was sold to Delfont Mackintosh Theatres, then after *Billy Elliot* ended its run in April 2016 it closed for a multi-million-pound refurbishment. In December 2017 the Broadway musical *Hamilton* reopened the refurbished Victoria Palace.

The London Hippodrome opened in 1900, designed by Frank Matcham as a circus variety theatre. It once featured a 100,000-gallon tank in which polar bears and sea lions would swim. Work in 1909 enlarged the stage and advanced the proscenium to suit the theatre for variety rather than circus use and, from 1912, revue-style performances. Innumerable famous artists have trodden its stage.

In the 1950s the Hippodrome was transformed into the legendary Talk of the Town, and featured a host of major stars including Shirley Bassey, Judy Garland, Bruce Forsyth, Sammy Davis Junior, The Jackson Five and Tom Jones.

After various different reincarnations, including a nightclub under the management of Peter Stringfellow, the theatre returned to its grass roots in 2009. It presented a final vaudeville revue called *La Clique*, which closed in June 2009. The opening of the Casino marked a new beginning for the Hippodrome, and it certainly retains its Victorian splendour, though unfortunately they won't be raising the tabs any more.

Above: The current exterior of the London Hippodrome. *Courtesy of the Hippodrome Casino*

Left: This programme documents Max Bygraves's appearance at the London Hippodrome. *Author's collection*

Frankie Howard and Barbara Windsor top the bill at the Hackney Empire. *Courtesy of Hackney Empire*

The Hackney Empire was one of the main music halls in London's East End, attracting acts from all over the world. The Empire opened in 1901 and featured some of the biggest music hall names of the time. A local cockney girl, Marie Lloyd, graced the stage and so did Stanley Holloway, Charlie Chaplin, W. C. Fields and Stan Laurel.

The variety industry slowly died in the 1950s, and the theatre was purchased by the ATV television company. Changing fortunes led to the Hackney Empire becoming a bingo hall run by Mecca in the 1960s. The building was given a Grade II listing incurred high renovation costs.

The theatre became the permanent

Above and right: The Hackney Empire. *Courtesy of the Hackney Empire*

Frank Matcham: Theatre architect extraordinaire

base of what was to become the main alternative comedy circuit in London, but by 1986 there was a real threat that it would be demolished and redeveloped. Correspondingly a campaign was started to save it. The company that owned the historic theatre established the Hackney Empire Preservation Trust and the Hackney New Variety Management Company to help manage the project.

In 2001 the management set in place a massive restoration project that was part funded by donations. The theatre was completely refurbished and renovated and did not reopen again until 2004.

The Hackney Empire is one of five surviving London theatres that characterise Frank Matcham's architectural craft and is still open for business for plays, ballet and opera performances as well as the Christmas panto, and long may it remain so.

The Richmond Theatre at Richmond upon Thames is another glorious example of the work of theatre architect Frank Matcham. It had taken only 12 months to build at a cost of £30,000. Writing in 1982, the theatre historian John Earl described it as being 'of outstanding importance as the most completely preserved Frank Matcham theatre in Greater London, and one of the most satisfying interiors.' The theatre is Grade II listed by English Heritage.

The theatre, originally known as the Theatre Royal and Opera House, is structured into the familiar stalls, dress and upper circles, with four boxes at dress level. The auditorium is a mixture of gilt detailing and red plush fabrics, covering the seats and the frontage of the circles. The ornate ceiling portrays four scenes from Shakespeare's plays: *King Lear*, *Hamlet*, *A Midsummer Night's Dream* and *Romeo and Juliet*.

The Richmond Theatre opened on 18 September 1899 with a performance of Shakespeare's *As You Like It*.

During the first two decades of the 20 century famous music

The statue standing atop the theatre is one of the Greek Muses, mythological goddesses inspiring art, science and literature. *Courtesy of Nick Simpson*

Above and below: Views of the interior of this classic Matcham theatre. All *Courtesy of Nick Simpson*

Frank Matcham: Theatre architect extraordinaire

hall acts, epitomised by Lillie Langtry, Marie Lloyd, Stan Laurel, Ellen Terry and, in 1921, Gracie Fields, all played the Richmond Theatre, and many of Britain's greatest actors have also graced the stage.

The elegant theatre has an out-of-town feel despite being just 20 minutes from Waterloo station. In fact, music hall stars used to do a matinee performance at the Richmond Theatre before returning by train to the West End to do an evening performance.

In the early 1990s the theatre underwent a major overhaul, and is now part of the Ambassador Theatre Group presenting plays and musicals.

Buxton Opera House was built in 1903, and another of Frank Matcham's designs. It ran as a successful theatre, receiving touring companies until 1927, when it was turned into a cinema projecting silent films. In 1932 the theatre began presenting the first talkies, and it survived until it fell into disrepair and went permanently dark in 1976.

In 1979, however, it was restored for stage productions, presenting opera, musicals, drama and concerts. The same year the Opera House and theatre complex became the home of the

The theatre opened on 18 September 1899 with Shakespeare's *As You Like It*.

Above and right: The beautiful Buxton Opera House.

Buxton Summer Festival and the Buxton Festival Fringe, an event that has developed into one of Britain's largest opera-based festivals.

In recent years an extensive programme of internal and external restoration has been undertaken. Fortunately this prime example of Matcham's work, with a seating capacity of 902, survives to delight audiences from Britain and abroad.

The Theatre Royal, Wakefield was a Matcham design of 1894, built at a cost of £13,000, and opening as the Wakefield Opera House.

In the 1920s the theatre competed with cinema by showing silent films, but with the advent of the talkies live shows were replaced by a season of films during the summer months. In 1954 the theatre became a cinema and a few years later a bingo hall. However, in 1981 it reopened as the Wakefield Theatre Royal under chairman Sir Rodney Walker, with support from artists and city leaders to revitalise the theatre. Today it operates as both a producing and a receiving house with a laudable mission statement: 'To develop new creative opportunities and experiences both within the theatre building, throughout the wider community and on tour, encouraging high-quality engagement across a broad sector of the Performing Arts.'

Wakefield's Theatre Royal is the smallest surviving example of Matcham's theatres and is a real gem.
Courtesy of Rob Booker and Paul White (auditorium)

Frank Matcham: Theatre architect extraordinaire

The Bristol Hippodrome, with seating on three levels, has an audience capacity of 1,951. The Hippodrome was designed by Frank Matcham for Oswald Stoll and opened on 16 December 1912. It is nowadays designated as a Grade II listed building.

An important feature of the theatre when it opened was a huge moveable water tank at the front of the stage, which

Above: Bristol Hippodrome auditorium and boxes. *Photos courtesy of Andy Phillips*

Left: The Bristol Hippodrome of yesteryear.

could be filled with 100,000 gallons of water. Together with the tank was a large protective glass screen, which could be raised in order to protect the orchestra and those in the stalls.

In 1947 a fire destroyed the stage area, though fortunately the theatre was reopened about 10 months later. The stage is now one of the largest outside London and is therefore capable of taking all the top West End touring musicals, a Christmas pantomime, and regularly plays host to Welsh National Opera.

Grand Opera House, Belfast: This theatre opened on 23 December 1895, as another classic Frank Matcham creation. In the early years it featured traditional music hall, comedy and drama, and in 1933 Gracie Fields played to a sold-out audience. During the Second World War in 1945 General Dwight Eisenhower with Field Marshal Montgomery watched a repertory performance here.

The end of the war brought opera and ballet and variety acts, some of which featured George Formby and Laurel and Hardy. In 1963 an unknown Italian singer named Luciano Pavarotti made his UK debut on the stage of the Grand Opera House as Lieutenant

The interior of the Grand Opera House, Belfast. *Photos courtesy of Chris Heaney (interior) and Brian Thompson (exterior)*

Frank Matcham: Theatre architect extraordinaire

Pinkerton in *Madame Butterfly*.

However, civil unrest took hold of Northern Ireland in 1969 and the city centre became a no-go area at night. By 1972 Rank, which had bought the Grand Opera House, had taken the decision to close the theatre and sell it to property developers. A campaign to save the building was launched and in 1974 it was designated a listed building.

Between 1976 and 1980 the Grand Opera House was extensively restored, including restoration of the ceiling panels in the main auditorium, but then disaster struck. In 1991 and again in 1993 the building suffered extensive damage following two car bombs in Glengall Street. Major refurbishment work followed both incidents, and today the theatre continues to prosper with hit shows from London's West End.

Theatre Royal, Newcastle-upon-Tyne: Granted its Royal licence by King George III, the Theatre Royal opened on Drury Lane, off Mosley Street, in 1788 and soon established itself as one of England's leading theatres. In February 1837 the theatre moved to Grey Street and the original building was demolished.

The Theatre Royal has a long and involved history involving many scene changes, changes of ownership, major renovations and serious fires. How ironic that following a performance of William Shakespeare's play *Macbeth* in 1899 a huge fire destroyed the interior of the building. The entire auditorium was redesigned by Matcham, but externally the building is exactly as it was when it was first built.

Over the centuries many of the great names of the English stage have played at the Royal, from Keane to Irving and Olivier to Dench, while the Hollywood greats Orson Welles, Charlton Heston and Jack

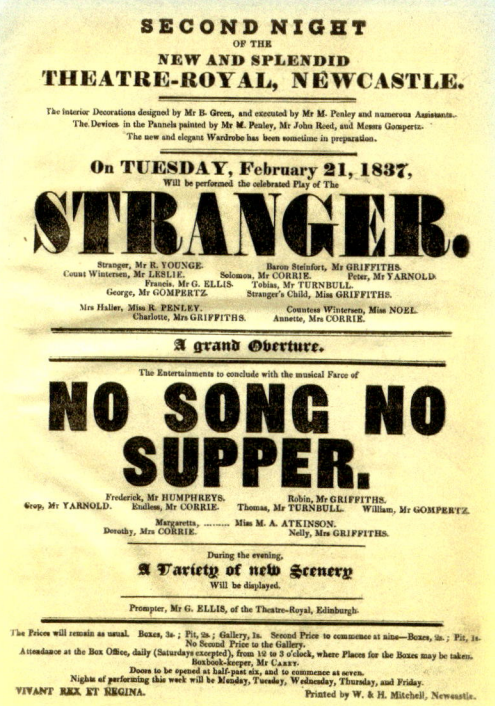

Left: The playbill for the second night of the reopened Theatre Royal, Newcastle, in February 1837. *Courtesy of Sally Ann Norman*

Right: The magnificent façade of Newcastle's Theatre Royal is generally regarded as the finest in the UK. *Courtesy of Sally Ann Norman*

Not surprisingly the Theatre Royal is one of the few Grade I listed theatres in England. *Courtesy of Sally Ann Norman*

Lemmon have also trodden the famous boards. Sir Ian McKellen has described the Theatre Royal as his favourite theatre.

The theatre went dark on 14 March 2011 for a major restoration of the auditorium, box office, bars and restaurant. Complete with its five distinct seating areas – stalls, grand circle, upper circle, amphitheatre and gallery reaching aloft to the gods – the restoration has restored the awesome building to its original Edwardian splendour.

Today the Theatre Royal hosts more than 300 performances every year, presenting the finest drama, the brightest West End musicals, the cream of the comedy circuit, award-winning ballet and dance, family friendly shows, sensational opera and one of the best pantomimes in the country!

His Majesty's Theatre, Aberdeen opened in 1906 with the panto *Little Red Riding Hood*. It is an awe-inspiring Matcham-designed theatre, with a breathtaking auditorium described by Billy Connolly as 'like playing a gig inside

Frank Matcham: Theatre architect extraordinaire

a wedding cake!' Like most surviving Matcham theatres, it is a national treasure.

Throughout its existence, His Majesty's Theatre has gone through three major refurbishments to keep up with the ever-changing demands of the entertainment industry. The theatre seats around 1,470 people and was reopened in September 2005 following a major £8 million redevelopment that successfully added a modern aspect to the historic Edwardian building. The new facilities have brought the theatre to life, offering 21st-century theatregoers a truly memorable experience. The Aberdeen theatre

His Majesty's Theatre is one of only two so named in the world, the other being in Perth, Australia. *Courtesy of Aberdeen Performing Arts Archive*

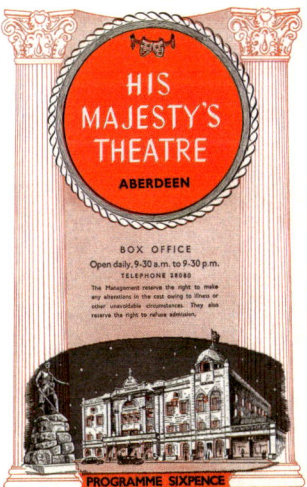

A programme from His Majesty's Theatre. *Author's collection*

presents top West End musicals, Scottish opera and ballet, acclaimed stage plays, internationally renowned contemporary dance, and a Christmas pantomime.

His Majesty's Theatre is steeped in history and a visit is highly recommended.

Edinburgh Festival Theatre (formerly the Empire): Edinburgh's Empire Palace Theatre was the first of the Moss Empire's chain of variety theatres to open, on 7 November 1892. It was also, in 1896, the first in Scotland to present the Lumière Brothers' moving pictures. Matcham's decor was lavish and it originally seated 3,000 people on four levels.

However, its early history is dominated by a tragic fire that occurred on Tuesday 9 May 1911, when 11 people died. The world-renowned illusionist and magician The Great Lafayette was top of the bill and more than 3,000 spectators had come to see him. As The Great Lafayette took his bow, a gas lamp fell towards the scenery, which immediately set the highly inflammable material ablaze. The fire safety curtain saved the auditorium and all customers managed to escape. Tragically the same could not be said for The Great Lafayette and backstage staff, who had been trapped behind the curtain.

Moss Empires had the theatre rebuilt again to the designs of its original architect, Frank Matcham, and it reopened within a matter of months with a succession of famed stars such as ballerina Anna Pavlova, impersonator Vesta Tilley, and comic actors Charlie Chaplin and Laurel and Hardy. The Empire continued in this form as a variety theatre for the next 17 years, but was replaced by a completely new theatre in 1928.

By now the theatre was simply known as the Empire and presented variety, musicals, operas and ice shows until 1963. Nonetheless, the variety theatre then began to follow a familiar pattern when it was converted into a bingo hall, known as the New Empire Casino. Fortuitously in June 1994 the old Empire façade was exchanged for a contemporary glass-fronted design with the auditorium retained and enhanced. Today the prestigious Edinburgh Festival Theatre offers top-class dance and opera and occasional large-scale music events.

Both success and tragedy has been a feature of the Empire Festival Theatre throughout its long and fascinating history, and the tragic events of 9 May 1911 are a significant part of that history. Backstage tours are available to those who wish to delve further.

King's Theatre, Glasgow, another Matcham design, is one of Scotland's most historic and significant theatres, opening in 1904. With a seating capacity of 1,785, it is Glasgow's largest theatre and has seen Scottish and international stars. Famous

Edinburgh Festival Theatre. *Courtesy of Capital Theatres*

Frank Matcham: Theatre architect extraordinaire

names appearing have included Michael Caine, Tyrone Power, Laurence Olivier, Katherine Hepburn, Stanley Baxter and Michael Jackson.

The Theatre hosts the Glasgow International Comedy Festival, top musicals and an annual Christmas pantomime. There is always a healthy rivalry with other Scottish theatres to put on the biggest and best Christmas pantomimes; the main competition is now the Pavilion Theatre, a former music hall, in Renfield Street.

The theatre provides seating on four levels – stalls, grand circle, upper circle and gallery. In 2002 day-to-day management was transferred to the Ambassador Theatre Group, becoming the group's first venue in Scotland. The theatre continues to present first-class musicals and pantomime alongside a wider range of drama, dance and comedy.

Left and above: Glasgow's Kings Theatre, affectionately known as 'The Grand Old Lady of Bath Street', is a Grade A listed building that has influences of art nouveau and baroque throughout its design. *Gordon McKerracher*

Chapter Five – London's magnificent Coliseum

For me, the grandest and largest theatre in the West End, the Coliseum Theatre in St Martin's Lane, is the magnum opus of the work of Frank Matcham. The Roman imagery complete with chariots is awe-inspiring and just like a scene from the film *Ben-Hur*. Therefore I devote this chapter to London's magnificent Coliseum.

Frank Matcham developed close relationships with theatre owners, especially Sir Oswald Stoll, for whom he designed his supreme masterpiece, the London Coliseum Theatre of Varieties, in 1904. This became the flagship venue for Matcham's chain of theatres and music halls and the largest and finest 'people's palace of entertainment' of the age. Matcham wanted a theatre of variety – not a music hall but equally not highbrow entertainment. The theatre's original slogan was PRO BONO PUBLICO ('for the public good').

Sir Oswald Stoll's opening of the Coliseum in December 1904 first made music hall respectable enough for a man to visit with his wife. The entertainment was renamed 'variety' and the Coliseum opened as a variety theatre; to this day it epitomises the grandeur of the Edwardian variety theatre.

At the time of its construction the Coliseum was the only theatre in Europe to provide lifts for taking patrons to the grand circle, upper circle and balcony. It was the first theatre in England to have a triple revolve installed on its stage, although this was rarely used. The stage consisted of three concentric rings, was 75 feet across in total, and cost Stoll £70,000. A range of modern features included not only the electric lifts, but also a roof garden and an information bureau in which physicians or others expecting urgent telephone calls or telegrams could leave their seat numbers and be immediately informed if required. The

London's magnificent Coliseum architecture heightens the London skyline. *Courtesy of ENO*

Coliseum has the widest proscenium arch in London (55 feet wide and 34 feet high); the stage is 80 feet wide, with a throw of more than 115 feet from the stage to the back of the balcony). With 2,359 seats it has the largest seating capacity of any theatre in London.

After 1945 the theatre was used for variety shows, musical comedies and stage plays. In 1961 it became a cinema for seven years, screening films in the Cinerama format. In 1968 it reopened as The London Coliseum, home of Sadler's Wells Opera. In 1974 Sadler's Wells became English National Opera and the Company

London's magnificent Coliseum

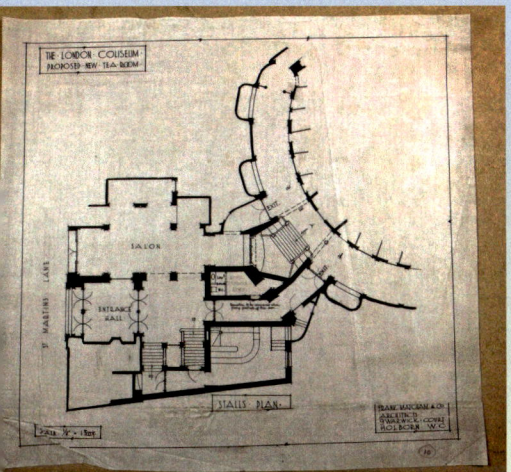

Above: Frank Matcham's original architectural plans for the Coliseum. *Courtesy of ENO*

Below and right: The magnificent Coliseum's auditorium. *Courtesy of ENO*

purchased the freehold of the building for £12.8 million in 1992.

The Coliseum underwent extensive renovations between 2000 and 2004, which were supported by the National Heritage Lottery Fund and English Heritage. The auditorium and other public areas were returned to their original Edwardian decoration and new public spaces were created. The theatre reopened in 2004.

Sadler's Wells Theatre, Islington, moved to the London Coliseum in 1968 and adopted its present name, English National Opera (ENO), in 1974. The company is one of the world's most innovative and accessible opera companies, with an international reputation for distinctive, contemporary and highly theatrical productions. ENO is one of two principal opera companies in London, the other being the Royal Opera, Covent Garden. The company has aimed to present the standard operatic repertoire, sung in English, and has staged all the major operas of Mozart, Wagner and Puccini, together with a wide range of Verdi's operas.

Today the renowned theatre, affectionately known in the trade as 'the colly', is used for opera and occasional musicals, as well as being the London home of English National Ballet.

Chapter Six – The bread and butter circuit

The Broadhead Syndicate

During the early 20th century, Moss Empires, Stoll, Howard and Wyndham were the major touring syndicates offering variety and pantomime. In contrast, the Broadhead circuit was a Manchester-based local and regional syndicate, known colloquially in the trade as the 'bread and butter circuit'. After the Boer War theatres were getting back into profit, and a niche for music hall in Manchester and throughout Lancashire was exploited by the Broadhead syndicate. They had the financial resources to exploit the growing music hall industry.

The business began when William Birch Broadhead first managed to persuade his father, William Henry Broadhead, to invest his capital in a theatre in Manchester. He earmarked some sites and in 1895 the first to be built was the Royal Osborne in Oldham Road. Subsequently 13 halls were erected in Manchester and at Bury, Ashton-under-Lyne, Eccles, Liverpool, Manchester, Preston and Salford. In 1909 Broadhead acquired the Winter Gardens, Morecambe, and three years later the Lyceum Theatre, Eccles. Influenced by Frank Matcham, William Birch designed most of the theatres, and the person responsible for interpreting his ideas was Mr J. J. Allen, who was an architect employed by W. H. Broadhead & Sons. The building and contracting department was based in Manchester.

The Broadhead Repertory Players performed across the circuit. Melodrama was staged at the Royal Osborne Theatre, Manchester (1895), the Metropole (1898) and the Grand Junction (1901). The Hulme Hippodrome and adjoining Grand Junction music hall were built as 'vast palaces of amusement' for Hulme residents.

The Broadheads grasped that dramatic productions and a range of eclectic entertainment, especially variety, was a marketable proposition. Their motto for variety interest was 'make it quick, clean, smart and bright'. The circuit was known to acrobats, comics, glamorous dancing girls, magicians, vocalists and a plethora of music hall entertainers as the 'bread and butter' tour because regular bookings did not produce the high wages of the Moss Empire and Howard and Wyndham circuits. The average wage of artists during the Edwardian period would be

The Broadhead family was instrumental in building 14 theatres, mainly in working-class areas of Manchester. Author's collection

The bread and butter circuit

about £5-10 per week and after paying for fares and living expenses they would not have had much cash left over.

Broadhead's talent scout Ernest Sims had the job of watching artists' performances and, if they were found to be suitable, they were booked with a wage that was guaranteed while they toured Broadhead's huge music halls. Syndicate management and the development of theatrical agents meant that stars could be booked across a network of halls. The artists developed their act by judging the level of enthusiasm from audiences in case they ever graduated to the Moss Empires syndicate of variety theatres. At the Glasgow Empire artists knew they would have to suffer an onslaught of verbal abuse, not to mention well-aimed tomatoes, if their act did not go down well!

William Henry Broadhead and his sons played a major role in the establishment of music hall in the North West. He had started life as a builder in Mansfield, but later in life ill health had forced him to relocate, so in 1883 he had moved to a 'famous seaside town called Blackpool, noted for fresh air and fun.'

Throughout a long business career Broadhead's business policy was to anticipate and react to change, and this was very much a hallmark of the management of their theatres. The firm knew how to make money and William Henry (the management) toured his theatres in a Daimler limousine. At his home on the promenade in Blackpool, the 'returns' from all his theatres were sent for scrutiny, and were usually opened with a special paper knife by one of his grandchildren.

Broadhead built Preston's Royal Hippodrome in 1905, in less than eight months without modern construction

The famed Broadhead theatrical family built up an empire throughout North West England, where artists likely travelled on the 'bread and butter' circuit behind steam engines like this 'Jubilee' No 45692 and Fairburn tank No 42135, both seen here south of Lancaster. *Noel Machell*

equipment. Backstage the height of the flies was restricted by the reduced gable end and there was a lack of space for painting and building scenery. Such frugal and skimpy conditions may have been based on the Broadhead philosophy that, in case of poor box office 'returns', all theatres could be redesigned for use as factories– this was at the height of the industrial revolution though, and neither of Broadhead's Preston theatres had to resort to this. The Royal Hippodrome theatre opened on 16 January 1905, managed by J. Freeman, who came from Broadhead's Queen's Park Hippodrome, Manchester.

A special variety programme had been arranged and top of the bill was Charles Coburn, singing 'The man who Broke the Bank at Monte Carlo' and 'Two Lovely Black Eyes', which were fully appreciated. There were good houses at both performances in the evening. The prospering music hall industry and the Broadhead contribution to it was acknowledged by the performer Percy Honri, who once said that 'W. H. Broadhead & Sons were builders of theatres rather than bidders for theatres someone else had built'.[18]

During the 1920s William Henry resisted an offer of a quarter of a million pounds from a film distributor wanting to purchase the whole chain of theatres as cinema outlets. His son Percy persuaded him that he was the only man in the country personally to own 17 theatres and he should retain them. It was resolved that Broadhead's magnificent halls for the delectation of the people would be around a little longer, but sadly time was also running out for the creator of the Broadhead circuit.

William Henry died in 1931 at the age of 83, and most of his theatres were sold by auction in 1932. A substantially reduced Broadhead tour was now managed by his grandchildren, Percy Baynham Broadhead Junior, also known as Sonny Broadhead, and Avril Broadhead. This lasted until the closure of the King's Palace, Preston and a few months later, the Salford Royal Hippodrome in 1955, trends that were by no means exclusive to provincial music hall.

Respectable audiences and twice-nightly performances

The response by Victorian theatre and music hall proprietors to counter their critics was to adopt and internalise the principles of respectability in audiences, especially throughout the period 1864-1904. Hence class consciousness and respectability were all the rage in Edwardian Britain! Respectability was the keyword for all classes and, unlike the Victorian music hall, reliance on alcohol as a source of funding was less important.

From the first performance, the Broadhead traditions had to be strictly followed. Staff had to be 'shiningly' clean and immaculately dressed and live up to the catchphrase 'on the ball', uttered by the manager of one of the theatres, Walter Hume. Before opening he paraded all the staff dealing with the public and inspected their hands, nails and general appearance. Walter maintained that the box office staff and programme-seller's faces and hairstyles must be up to the standard expected by patrons at that time.

The insistence on making theatre staff look very smart lends some support to Russell's view that there was an attempt to attract a wider social class strata in music hall post 1890:

'There is implicit evidence that from the 1890s significant sections of the middle class began to attend, encompassing clerks, teachers, managers and even some professionals with their families.'[19]

By 1904 audiences were increasingly bound by the behavioural constraints of respectability. The promotion of respectable forms of recreation led to music hall

The bread and butter circuit

'Let's all go to the music hall by charabanc!'

proprietors again adopting the rhetoric of respectability as a defensive strategy.

There is evidence of programming that aimed to add refinement to entertainment, and of propaganda from proprietors designed to counter possible condemnation and therefore to attract larger audiences from the middle class. W. H. Broadhead & Sons maintained that the respectable citizen could take his wife and children to any of its productions, find them free from vulgarity and at a price well within his means.

Part of their concept of respectability in their theatres was to bring greater diversity of programming for audiences in variety theatres, with 'dramatic productions of an uplifting moral nature' at prices they could afford.

The King's Palace

The last of Broadhead's theatres to be built was the King's Palace at Preston. William Henry Broadhead, proclaimed:

'Another Messrs Broadhead & Sons achievement in the raising of magnificent halls for the delectation of the people. This is the most up-to-date theatre in Lancashire offering opera from the Grand Junction, Manchester, and pantomime from the Pavilion, Liverpool.'[20]

A diminishing music hall genre at the King's Palace between 1913 and 1917 is apparent. During 1917 it advertised: 'One continuous performance come what time you like stay as long as you like.' After 1917 it sustained regular cinema use interspersed with occasional stage shows before reverting to a full-time commercial live theatre in the 1930s.

As television began to grasp the nation's attention, the King's Palace, with an audience capacity of almost 3,000, was playing to houses of only 20 to 50 patrons. Attempts to keep it open with striptease simply drove the family audiences away, and such wretched performances were fatalistic in a melancholy way.

Raise a laugh with unscripted performances

In the early 1950s the Great Levant performed his illusionist variety act at the King's Palace. His glamorous lady assistant was placed in a trunk and, and after numerous stabbings of the trunk with swords, the trunk would normally be found to be empty. The assistant would then appear from the rear of the stalls to take her bow, or at least that was the theory. But the assistant had gone AWOL and was unable to find the stage door entrance from the street outside. It was pouring with rain, but nevertheless she eventually reappeared on stage looking extremely wet in her skimpy costume. While waiting, the Great Levant had to resort to a considerable amount of ad-libbing, which was quite out of character.

Another debacle staged at the Palace was Koringa and Friends. Her act was

THE LANCASHIRE DAILY POST, THURSDAY, FEBRUARY 6, 1913.

THE NEW KING'S PALACE

THEATRE, Old Vicarage, and Tithebarn Street, Preston.

PROPRIETORS — WILLIAM HENRY BROADHEAD AND SON.

6-40 | Thursday, Friday, & Saturday, FEBRUARY 6th, 7th, & 8th, 1913 | Second House, 9.0

CHARLES BARNOLD'S

TALENTED

DOG and MONKEY ACTORS

IN A ONE ACT COMEDY PANTOMIME

"A HOT TIME IN DOGVILLE,"

INTRODUCING

"DAN," the Drunken Dog,

WHOSE CLEVER ACTING CREATES ROARS OF LAUGHTER

A WONDERFUL EXAMPLE OF CANINE INTELLIGENCE.

Harry Taft

THE FAMOUS AMERICAN WHISTLING COMEDIAN.

Will Douglas & Co.

IN A COMEDY CONCOCTION, "THE MERRY DEMONS."

Donald & Carson

J. W. Winton

THE AUSTRALIAN VENTRILOQUIST.

The FOUR MUSICAL GARDINERS

AUSTRALIA'S GREATEST STARS.

HARVARD SEXTETTE,

IN MIRTH, MELODY, AND MOVEMENT.

JOHN TILLER'S FAMOUS

12 SUNSHINE GIRLS

DIRECT FROM THEIR ENORMOUS SUCCESSES AT THE WINTERGARTEN, BERLIN, AND AMERICAN TOUR.

OVERTURE, "WILLIAM TELL" (Rossini), STORM SCENE, MARCH MILITAIRE and GRAND FINALE, BY THE PALACE ORCHESTRA, under the Direction of ROBERT PEEL.

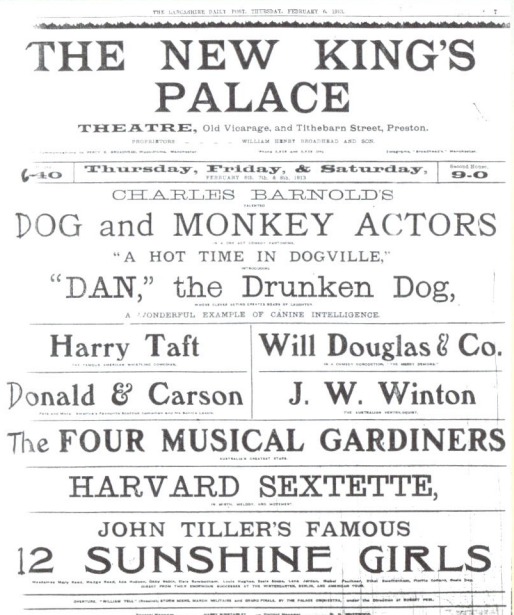

The opening night programme for the brand new King's Palace Theatre, Preston, on Thursday 6 February 1913. *Author's collection*

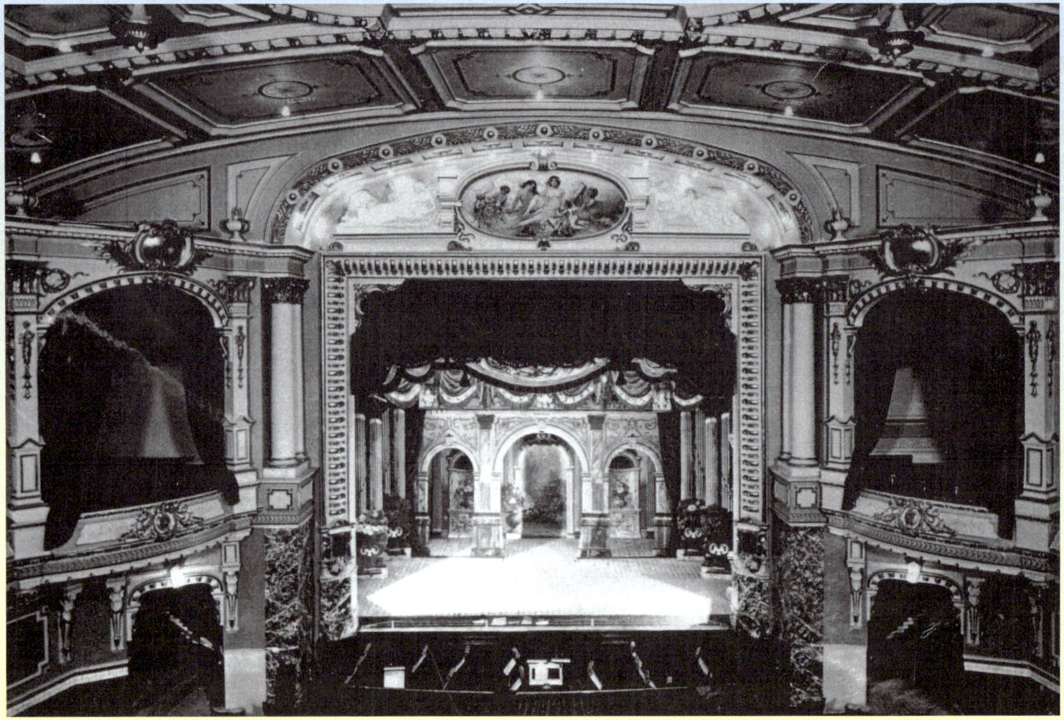

The new King's Palace at the time of opening in 1913. *Author's collection*

artfully crafted and drew on a number of influences that unfolded in music halls, fairgrounds and circuses. Koringa was an exotic circus and music hall performer who shocked her audience with a necklace of live snakes and her ability to walk on the heads of hypnotised crocodiles – or at least that was the theory.

But at the King's Palace the supposedly hypnotised crocodile took umbrage at the humiliation, bit Koringa's bottom and dropped into the orchestra pit. Although it may appear that the mystified crocodile had bitten off more than it could chew, it nevertheless led to a rapid exit of panicking musicians and a startled audience. Meanwhile the croc's mentor grabbed it by its tail and made a rapid exit stage left! Koringa was able to give the usual performance at the second house that same evening. Could this have been the precursor to modern health and safety legislation? Perhaps not!

It was always a proud boast of Broadhead that teenage Charlie Chaplin was among the cavalcade of famous artists that trod the boards of his circuit. However, daring escapologist and pioneer of stage magic, Harry Houdini, real name Eric Weisz, never forgot his visit to the Royal Hippodrome in 1906. He promoted his act by first visiting HM Prison, Preston, to uphold his reputation that no lock, straightjacket or prison could ever hold him. He almost lost the challenge after finding that the prison had unusual locks and handcuffs, and it took him three hours to set himself free. He injured his hands in making the escape and recorded his thanks to the young doctor who treated him. He

The King's Palace presented Miss Hetty King in May 1937, and a cavalcade of adverts. Admission prices ranged from 6d to 3 shillings. *Author's collection*

said afterwards: 'Preston should be equally proud of its prison as its North End football team. Your prison is one of the most secure places I have ever come across.' Later he wrote in his diary that Preston was one of the best places he had visited, even though he almost lost his international reputation here. While not reported at the time, rumour has it that once in the cell he wasn't making much progress until one of the guards told him what was on the tea menu in 1906. This message introduced the necessary urgency, and within the hour he was walking out of the prison!

No theatre can be without the story of a theatre ghost, and this one gets intermittent star billing – now you see him, now you don't! In January 1913 Alman Correge and his partner, John Smith, were presenting their comedy juggling act. John's part of the routine was to throw himself all over the stage, and trip over the props. Towards the end of the act it was his custom to lie down at the edge of the stage and pretend he was asleep. One night he commenced a very long sleep indeed, and, when the curtain was raised for them to take a bow, he didn't spring up on his feet. The audience thought it was all part of the act, but he was carried off and the resident police constable, William Hamer, who always sat at the back of the stalls to check that no offensive actions or words were portrayed, was called to the stage door to administer first aid.

Sadly, poor John was already dead from natural causes. True to theatrical traditions, the show carried on and so did John Smith, even after having shuffled off this mortal coil. He always smoked cigars and audiences often commented on the unusual aroma, especially cigar smoke, that permeated the auditorium.

The end was inevitable and, due to hard times, the King's Palace closed on Saturday 19 February 1955. *Courtesy of Lancashire Evening Post*

The bread and butter circuit

Roy Barraclough.

Roy Barraclough recalls the music halls of his home town

In 1999 star of *Coronation Street* and traditional panto dame Roy Barraclough, of 'Cissie and Ada' variety fame with Les Dawson, kindly wrote the following for my book *Twice Nightly*:

'The Palace was Preston's old variety theatre and I remember being taken by my parents to see the pantomime and, when they thought it was suitable, to see the variety bills. I clearly recall the speciality acts – the lady who walked the tightrope from the stage up to the gallery holding a rather faded parasol, then slid all the way back from the roof to the footlights (a most daring stunt, I thought), the man on the motorbike whirling round inside a metal globe, the man who conducted electricity with his body in order to light a bulb … just wonderful!

Later in my teens, Hylda Baker, Norman Evans, Jimmy James, Sandy Powell, George Robey (whom I never liked), Vesta Tilley, Robb Wilton and Frank Randle (whom I thought was by far the funniest comic) all appeared there. Then, just like legitimate theatre, with the advent of television it began to die. Strip shows took their place with titles such as 'Peaches and Screams', 'Who Goes Bare?' and of course 'Soldiers in Skirts', with a very young Danny La Rue. Eventually the Palace was closed and pulled down too, another loss to Preston.'

And a final word from the author

My parents took me along to the pantomime performances at Preston's two live theatres. As a four-year-old I was scared stiff of the big bad wolf in *Little Red Riding Hood*, especially when the woodcutter beheaded the wolf – gruesome stuff, so count me out for this act at the Kings Palace!

I'm told that the last performance in February 1955 was a revue called 'Peaches and Screams', starring a veteran of the variety stage, emaciated comedian without teeth, Ted Lune. The owner of the Palace, he and Percy 'Sonny' Broadhead went on stage and announced its closure before leaving it to Ted to entertain the audience for an extended show, which lasted until well after midnight. Ted's catchphrase, 'Throw me the keys, I'll lock up,' suddenly took on a particular poignancy for the audience and staff watching this last performance.

Sir Ken Dodd once told me that he never played the King's Palace at Preston, but he wished that he had. He did play Preston's Charter Theatre, and in 1999 I was given the opportunity to show him my first book about Preston music hall, *Twice Nightly*. I was pleased when he responded with the words, 'Oh, I love books like that, I'll have one of them.' I felt honoured to present him with a copy and in exchange he gave me a signed photograph and signed my own copy of *Twice Nightly*.

During 1964 I sat in the stalls of the now demolished Preston Empire Theatre, a former music hall that closed in 1930 and became a cinema, to watch Sigmund

Left and below left: The King's Palace and Royal Hippodrome theatres, Preston, both staged traditional panto, as seen here in 1939 and 1953.
Author's collection

Right: The Preston Empire at the time of opening.
Drawing by Christine Dodding

Below: The Student Prince was staged for one week only, during May 1964, after the theatre had been used as a cinema for 34 years.
Author's collection

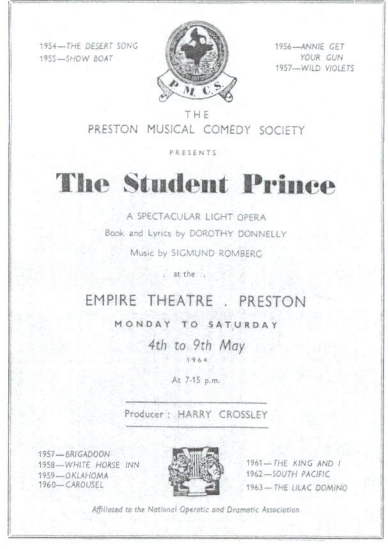

Romberg's spectacular light opera *The Student Prince*. I shared the experience with my Grandma Bowman, who remembered the shows at the Empire of long ago.

This window of opportunity arose when Preston Musical Comedy Society persuaded the theatre management to reinstate the cinema as a theatre, to accommodate the production. 'Raise the tabs, maestro, take your cue.' The Empire was reborn as a live theatre from 4 to 9 May 1964, but the final awakening was for all too short a period. This was to be my very own journey into the history of Preston's entertainment industry to absorb the traditions of music hall and the variety theatre that was to inspire so much of my research.

Chapter Seven – Morecambe and Wise: Getting their act together on a train while touring the provinces

In this chapter the spotlight is focused firmly on the much-loved comic double act Morecambe and Wise. I have already described how the national railway network was pivotal to their career during the mid-20th century, while they were playing the major variety theatres of Britain. Eric Bartholomew OBE (14 May 1926-28 May 1984) and Ernest Wiseman OBE (27 November 1926-21 March 1999) toured the music halls for 25 years before becoming a national institution on British television.

Eric Bartholomew was born in the Lancashire seaside resort of Morecambe, where his mother Sadie worked as an usherette at Morecambe Winter Gardens. It was Sadie who became his mentor and inspiration for a career in show business. At the age of nine Eric was already performing in local talent shows at the Morecambe Odeon. Ironically he was subsequently banned as a candidate for being too good and coming first every time.

Sadie entered him for more talent contests and in 1939 he won the local leg of a nationwide competition organised by music magazine *Melody Maker*. The prize was an audition with the legendary Jack Hylton, whose shows were the top attraction of the day. Sitting with Hylton, as the 13-year-old Eric Bartholomew went through his act, was Hylton's latest child star – one Ernest Wiseman, a short, confident Leeds boy. It was the first time the future double act had laid eyes on each other and the initial signs were not promising. Of course, later on, when they toured together as individual acts, they became best friends, and in a way that was down to Sadie too.

Travelling by train and the birth of a comedy duo

Eric Bartholomew and Ernest Wiseman were only 13 and 14 respectively when they were spotted at a stage talent show doing their solo acts in Brian Michie's 'Youth Takes a Bow'. Their experience led to touring, with Eric's mother Sadie as their chaperone, although it was not until 1940 that Eric and Ernie first got thrown together as a double act. They had been working on the same bill as separate acts and were commuting around the country on the train with Sadie. During the war they were booked to play Coventry for a week, but Coventry was bombed unmercifully, with many guest houses being flattened. The show had to go on, however, so Sadie decided that they would stay in digs in Birmingham, and commute the 21 miles to Coventry by train each day.

During the train journey both teenagers were on a high and were chattering and joking non-stop. Having listened to their endless jokes and shared banter, Sadie suggested that they give up solo performances and become a double act, using new jokes and original material of their own. They both thought it was a good idea and at first they used the stage name Bartholomew and Wise.

The pair performed their double act for the first time at the Liverpool Empire in 1941 under the watchful eye of Jack Hylton. At this time it was suggested that Eric should take his name from his home town of Morecambe and that Ernie change from

Wiseman to Wise. So began the journey to stardom of comedy legends 'Morecambe and Wise,' a career that stayed on the rails, at least most of the time!

The boys were conscripted in 1943; Ernie went into the Merchant Navy, while Eric became a 'Bevin Boy', working in a coal mine in Accrington. After the war Sadie was determined that Morecambe and Wise should once again take to the stage. She acted as their agent throughout their early career, booking them gigs involving extensive train travel and organising theatre digs. Naturally the road to fame had its ups and downs. In 1947 they maintained their variety traditions by starring in a show called 'Lord Sanger's Circus and Variety'; after all, variety had its origins in music hall and circus, but Eric and Ernie found themselves at the foot of the variety bill. Their act was even billed below a flock of performing pigeons, with Eric carrying an advertising placard. Tea urn? No thank you!

On tour with variety acts in the can

For the majority of variety acts it was tough going – the non-stop rehearsals, the planning and finding of new acts to wow people – but for the comedian it was usually

Left and right: More steam-hauled trains captured at Galgate, south of Lancaster. In the early days of their career Morecambe and Wise would have travelled the country behind such locomotives. The first view (left) shows 'Jubilee' Class No 45701 on a down express, while the second (right) features a different double act, with Fairburn tank No 42457 and Stanier Class 5 No 45210, also heading north.
Noel Machell

The fabulous Liverpool Empire by night, where Morecambe and Wise first appeared in 1941.
Courtesy of Clare Jennings

Morecambe and Wise: Getting their act together on a train while touring the provinces

an easier life. They just walked onto the stage, did their routines and walked off again. That's why Eric and Ernie loved it.

Many comedians had the same act for years, touring around the nation's variety theatres on the train for more than two decades, meaning that the material never had to be changed. By the time they got back to the first theatre many years might have passed, and people would

Above and right: Travelling between the City Varieties at Leeds and Morecambe Winter Gardens might involve a former Midland Compound like this. No 41101 is seen here at Leeds City station, destination Morecambe. *Courtesy of Bob Gregson*

Right: Or travelling from the London Palladium to the Glasgow Empire might perhaps involve one of these. 'Coronation' Class No 46245 City of London heads a down 'Lakes Express' in circa 1960. *Courtesy of Bob Gregson*

have forgotten the jokes. Obviously the odd joke was added or taken away, but for the vast majority of music hall comedians their act remained the same for years.

From saucy revues to the London Palladium
Morecambe and Wise went onto perform at London's Windmill Theatre, famous for its striptease shows, though moving nudes were taboo – remember the adage: 'If it moves it's rude'. Nonetheless, they were spotted by an agent and secured a contract with the Moss Empire circuit, playing the best variety theatres in the country, which ultimately featured the renowned London Palladium. By 1950 the boys had secured a professional agent and within two years were regulars on the BBC radio show *Variety Fanfare*.

Above: Morecambe and Wise played many of the nation's theatres, such as the awe-inspiring Leeds Grand. *Courtesy of Leeds Grand Theatre and Opera House Ltd*

Below left and right: The Grand Theatre, Wolverhampton, is a huge asset to that city and its surrounding towns. *Courtesy of Jonathan Hipkiss*

It was only then that Sadie allowed herself to relax.

Touring the halls with Morecambe and Wise and the 'Old Dutch'
Morecambe and Wise spent 25 years treading the boards to earn a twice-nightly living, at first in provincial music halls. They later graduated to the top Moss Empire variety circuit embracing the prestigious

Above and right: Through the golden age of variety, a 1980s refurbishment and up to the present day, the Sheffield Lyceum has had a wonderful and varied history. Its Edwardian grandeur was the work of the theatre architect W. G. R. Sprague. *Courtesy of James Stewart*

London Palladium, not to mention the infamous Glasgow Empire. 'There's no business like show business', and naturally they co-starred with an eclectic range of music hall acts on the way.

One of the artists who regularly worked the Broadhead 'bread and butter' circuit and, later, Moss Empires was Jim Tattersall of Little Lever, Bolton. He too was a star of the music hall scene and starred alongside Morecambe and Wise at theatres throughout the country. I was privileged when Jim, the octogenarian retired trooper of Britain's music halls, granted me an audience. Jim was a past master in his original act of specialised ventriloquism, billed as Tattersall and Jerry. He manufactured his own life-sized dolls with their trademark goggle eyes. Apart from Jerry there was Old Joe and his dear wife, the 'Old Dutch.' During the act when Jim mentioned the 'Old Dutch' it was the cue for the maestro in the orchestra pit to strike up with the song 'We've been together now for forty years', and the 'Old Dutch' would walk across the stage to be serenaded by old Joe.

'Right, don't book your digs – I'll ring my Mum up'

Variety was one of the most popular forms of cheap entertainment throughout the first half of the twentieth century, and the railways carried public and performers alike around the country.

Early in his career Jim Tattersall got star billing with a comedy duo that was to become the nation's favourite double act, Morecambe and Wise. In those days Eric and 'Little Ern' did not have a car and toured the country by train. While working at the Sheffield Empire, Eric asked Jim, 'Where are you working next week'?

'Edinburgh,' came the reply.'

'Oh good – can we have a lift and pay half the cost of the petrol?'

On another occasion Eric repaid the favour when he asked, 'Where are you next week Jim?'

Jim responded, 'Winter Gardens, Morecambe.'

'Right,' said Eric, 'don't book your digs – I'll ring my Mum up!'

Jim worked alongside most of Britain's major stars, including Shirley Bassey, Peter Sellers Julie Andrews and the 'King of the Diddymen,' Ken Dodd, for whom he made several models, more especially his right-hand man, Diddy Mint.

The comic's graveyard

Jim, like Morecambe and Wise, graduated to the Moss Empire circuit of top British variety theatres, all staging twice-nightly performances with at least two matinees a week. The first of Jim Tattersall's engagements was the notorious Glasgow Empire, well known for the vitriolic candour and actions of a tough and raucous non-approving audience. The Glasgow Empire was known in the trade as the comic's graveyard, or the 'House of Terror', and, having survived a twice-nightly Saturday evening performance, Jim was brave enough to book a return visit.

It was a challenge too for Eric and Ernie, despite the extra £10 the Empire management paid them, ostensibly for the rail fare but strongly rumoured to be danger money. The stage manager told them not to forget to duck from an assortment of fruit hurled onto the stage, not altogether good for a performer's morale. After one evening performance the stage manager condescended a little encouragement: 'Did you hear that? Silence. They're beginning to like you.'

For poor Des O'Connor it was all too much and he fainted. Des was dragged under the curtains of the Empire so the audience could see the words 'Goodnight all' imprinted on the soles of his shoes.

Mike and Bernie Winters joined the ranks of those tormented at the Empire in their debut performance. Their act always began with Mike playing his clarinet, then

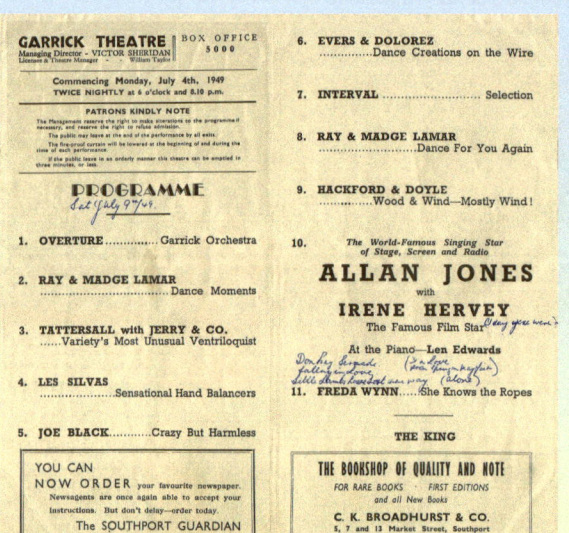

'Tattersall with Jerry and Co' are billed as 'Variety's Most Unusual Ventriloquist' at the Garrick, Southport, on Saturday 9 July 1949. *Author's collection*

shortly afterwards Bernie's goofy face would peek through the curtains only to be greeted by a voice from the Glasgow audience shouting, 'Christ, there's two of 'em!'

The Glasgow Empire closed in 1963 and an office block has been built on the site of the much-lamented theatre. It has been named Empire House, so any survivors of the variety theatre won't need to be reminded!

Recalling his career, Jim Tattersall told me: 'It was hard work, especially playing Glasgow Empire on a Friday and Saturday night. Nevertheless, there was something special about the old theatres, and those days have gone forever, but it was a fantastic life. I have a lot to thank the old Preston King's Palace for too – it gave me the break I was looking for.'

Meanwhile, at the Festival Theatre, Edinburgh, formerly the Empire, Eric met his future wife, a young singer called Joan Bartlett. They married on 11 December 1952. Ernie, too, married into the business with Doreen Blythe, also a dancer.

They did their first BBC TV show in 1953. Ronnie Waldman saw it, was impressed with their performance, and offered them a series of their own. The series, called *Running Wild*, was, in Eric and Ernie's own words, a 'disaster'. After the first show on 21 April 1954 it was given a right slating by the newspapers. The late Gilbert Harding said that watching the show felt like 'a snake transfixed by a rabbit'.

However, their television career got under way in the 1960s with performances on Val Parnell's *Sunday Night at the London Palladium* and later *The Morecambe and Wise Show* on ITV in 1961. The series topped TV popularity polls and went on to run for seven years. It brought them fame, not only in this country, but all over the world. They completed three major colour comedies for the Rank Organisation and travelled to America to appear regularly on *The Ed Sullivan Show*. They also had their own series, *Piccadilly Palace*, made in Britain by Lew Grade for screening in the United States.

Eric and Ernie switched channels to the BBC in 1968 and starred in the first colour series for British television on BBC2. Once again it was a tremendous success. The stars were now alternating between live theatre performances and television, and had achieved stardom, although it was a very busy life. They had hit the big time by the end of the Swinging Sixties and train travel was to be transformed into expensive cars. Michael Fountain became Eric's driver, friend and adopted member of the family from 1968. At that time Eric also had a Jensen Interceptor, the most expensive two-seater car of its time. In 1971 came the first Rolls-Royce Silver Shadow, then in 1974 came the brown Rolls-Royce Silver Shadow with the number plate EM 100.

During the 1970s Eddie Braben became their scriptwriters for ten years at the BBC. Morecambe and Wise were Britain's favourites, endorsed by the fact that their 1977 Christmas Day treat was watched by 28 million, an all-time record that still stands. *The Morecambe and Wise Christmas Show* became a tradition for millions across the nation, and featured top celebrities such as Glenda Jackson, Shirley Bassey, Andrew Previn, Tom Jones, Leonard Rossiter, Angela Rippon and a plethora of BBC newscasters, to name but a few, who sportingly joined in the gags. Eric and Ernie never forgot their links with music hall and fellow artists and friends, represented by the veteran performer Arthur Tolcher, who made brief appearances with a burst of harmonica, only to be told by Eric, in jocular fashion, 'Not now, Arthur.' In 1968 and 1978 Eric Morecambe suffered heart attacks, but fortunately recovered.

Eric the birdwatcher
Eric Morecambe was a keen fisherman and birdwatcher, the latter especially enjoyed with binoculars in hand in nice places away from the stage and his busy schedules. Eric returned to Morecambe occasionally, and one day I spotted him birdwatching while sitting comfortably in his car at Hest Bank, near his native seaside town. He seemed to be absorbed while watching the high tide wader roost, so I chose not to intrude on his privacy. But I need not have worried about asking Eric for this autograph and having a chat with him; Eric's driver informed me that his boss told him, 'If it wasn't for the general public I wouldn't be where I am today. They pay my wages.'

In 2007 I felt honoured when Mrs Joan Morecambe kindly wrote the Foreword to my book on *Bird Watching Walks Around Morecambe Bay*. She wrote:

'As a boy Eric loved the countryside and always took a keen interest in identifying and feeding the birds in and around his native Morecambe. In later years it became necessary for the sake of his health to take regular walks, which were made more absorbing by combining walks with birdwatching, when he could always be seen with binoculars at the ready. It is no surprise, therefore, that the wonderful statue of Eric (in familiar pose) which adorns Morecambe Promenade also has a pair of binoculars.

How thrilled he would have been to have had a lagoon and hide at the RSPB Leighton Moss and Morecambe Bay Nature Reserve named after him. We his family are delighted that the lagoon has proved such a success, especially now that avocets – the emblem of the RSPB, which he supported for many years – have taken to nesting there.

I am also delighted to have been asked to write this Foreword. As Eric knew very well, the area is rich in bird life and there are many beautiful walks during which it can be seen. It is a combination I know he would have enjoyed and I am sure that it will prove to be popular with walkers and birdwatchers from near and far.'

Remembering two great stars of the variety stage and television
For 40 years Ernie Wise was half of the greatest comedy double act in the history of British television. 'Little Ern' was the butt of Eric's jokes; he was the one with the 'short, fat, hairy legs', and Eric tormented him about his non-existent toupee with the words, 'You can't see the join'. Ernie delighted in boasting about 'the play what I wrote', while Eric asked, 'What do you think of it so far?' replying to himself with the word 'Rubbish!'

I will always remember them for their hilarious quips and banter, the famous celebrities and in particular that side-splitting sketch that embroiled their mentor Andrew Previn – or was it Privet … or Preview? Eric played the Grieg piano concerto in an amateurish way, causing the maestro to jump into the air and abandon his baton, leaving his symphony orchestra ostensibly perplexed. Meanwhile Eric sheepishly looked over the piano lid and explained, 'I am playing all the right notes … but not necessarily in the right order.'

High on the list of favourites for me was that trademark introductory song and dance routine, 'Bring Me Sunshine'. Certainly it was like a breath of fresh air as well as a ray of sunshine on millions of television sets.

Tragically in 1984 Eric suffered a fatal heart attack, at only 58 years old, and the nation lost a brilliant double act. Like others of his contemporaries – Arthur Lowe, Sid James, Leonard Rossiter and Tommy Cooper – Eric suffered his attack after finishing a live stage show, at the Roses

Theatre, Tewkesbury. He died enjoying what he did best. This left poor Ernie to rebuild his career. He became a television panellist on What's My Line? and appeared on stage as an actor in London's West End.

The Importance of Being Ernie (1993) reflected on the problems of facing up to life as a solo performer after years of endearing himself as half of a double act. 'We were ordained for each other,' said Ernie. 'I wouldn't have teamed up with anybody else, only Eric. It was like a marriage.'

Ernie died in Wexham, Buckinghamshire, on 21 March 1999.

The genuine article

Michael Fountain recalled his boss and good friend Eric in his book Driving Mr Morecambe. 'A question I am always asked is, "What was Eric like?" He was a star, but a star with both feet planted firmly on the ground, very down to earth, very intelligent and a great talker. He would go out of his way to please people, whether they were the director of a television network or a stranger in the street. To Eric they were his audience and he had to leave them laughing, and he always did. It didn't matter how he was feeling, it wasn't about him. He was compelled to make people happy, it was his duty and I think his destiny to entertain. He had been given this wonderful thing and he would use it at every opportunity, sometimes despite feeling very ill himself… He was a gentleman, a real gentleman, something sadly not seen very often these days. He didn't swear in front of ladies (or at all, really), he opened doors for people, he thought of others before himself, just a genuinely nice person. He didn't want to be the star, for him that concept didn't exist. He hated that side of the business. What you saw with Eric was what you got, the genuine article.' (Fountain, M. and Jenkinson, P. Driving Mr Morecambe (Authors on Line, 2013)

Behind every great man, so they say, is a great woman. And in the case of Eric Morecambe, once voted the funniest British star of the 20th century, that great woman was, his wife Joan and his Mum. Sadie always called him by his nickname, 'Sunshine', and 'Bring Me Sunshine' would later become Eric and Ernie's signature tune. From an early age Sadie was instrumental in both Eric entering show business and in the coming together of Eric and Ernie. Now sadly Eric and Ernie, their friends Tommy Cooper, Andre Previn ('Mr Preview') and the ventriloquist Jim Tattersall – not forgetting 'Old Dutch' – just like so many of their contemporaries, and the variety theatres themselves, have gone forever.

Unveiled by the Queen in 1999, the slightly larger-than-life-sized statue depicts Eric Morecambe in one of his characteristic poses with a pair of binoculars around his neck (he was a keen ornithologist). The statue is set against the stunning backdrop of Morecambe Bay and the Lake District hills, and people queue to have their photo taken alongside it.
Courtesy of Graham Wilkinson

Chapter Eight – The rise of cinema and decline of music hall

The Lumière brothers, Auguste Marie Louis Nicolas and Louis Jean, were among the first filmmakers in history. They gave their first paid public screening during December 1895 in Paris, with their patented improved cinematograph, and news of the technological breakthrough was soon widespread.

In 1897 a travelling fair at Hull featured cinematograph performances.[21] At Blackburn short films were shown at the travelling fairs from the mid-1890s and likewise at Preston. What was probably Preston's first embryonic cinema performance was reported in the *Preston Herald* on 12 June 1897 – a short film with an intriguing title 'The Lady Who Would Take a Bath'. This dubious event sounds somewhat naughty, though no doubt salacious in 1897.

In 1907 a journalist wrote in the trade paper, *The Encore*:

'Seven years ago I pointed out to the profession that the greatest enemies of the artistes were the film merchants. The cinematograph picture shows have come to stay, for each time an operator is employed two or three single turns are ousted.'

At first cinema was thought of as a minor item within the musical hall repertory, and billed as the bioscope, but it was not long before this accommodation was seen as competition. In March 1896 the Empire Theatre of Varieties, Leicester Square, played host to the first commercial theatrical performances of a projected film to a UK audience by Auguste and Louis Lumière. The film programme ran for 18 months. As moving pictures grew in popularity, the Empire became a cinema on 8 November 1928, and was subsequently acquired by Cineworld in July 2016 as a multi-screen cinema.

Music halls themselves began to introduce cinema into their programming, and between 1908 and 1914 cinemas presented variety acts on stage, a form known as cine-variety. The Palace Cinema at Longridge in Lancashire was originally a weaving shed and typifies the transition from music hall to cinema. The renowned Preston impresario, film-maker and circus performer Will Onda purchased the building in 1912 and opened it as a music hall with cine-variety.

Formerly served by the railway, it is one of the oldest cinemas in Lancashire and personifies the history of music hall and the combined smaller suburban cinema serving a local community. Cinemas grew in popularity and were a cheaper option than music hall and consequently the latter, like the Longridge Palace, were superseded by full-time cinema.

This unique cinema maintained old traditions and the playing of the National Anthem at the beginning of the film performance. However, in line with national social trends, few bridges would be built as the cinema impacted on music hall audiences. Before the First World War music halls were the main attraction, but as the silver screen began to have its own pulling power many theatres nationwide were adapted to show

The rise of cinema and decline of music hall

films. This led to the conversion of theatres and music halls, churches, warehouses and other buildings for cinema use, as well as the construction of the first purpose-built cinemas.

The first talkie featured Al Jonson in 1927. Throughout the next decade the phenomenon of the talkies brought a new batch of art-deco cinemas to towns and cities throughout Britain. Moreover, with the coming of the talkies established music hall stars like George Formby and Gracie Fields began to switch to cinema and made dozens of films during the 1930s. During the cinema boom of the 1940s and 1950s most cities, towns and seaside resorts had a plentiful number of cinemas. The talkies also brought some classic railway-themed films.

The biggest heroes of the working classes in post-war Britain were Gracie Fields and George Formby, and both were enormously popular in theatre, film, radio and on records. They were the embodiment of the native British popular culture during the 1930s, and both continued the tradition of working the halls, although they began to capitalise on their enormous popularity by starring in many films. 'Our Gracie' was an established music hall artist by the time of

Left: The Palladium Cinema, Preston, opened in 1915. The silent flickering pictures were to be succeeded by the talkies in the 1930s. *Lancashire Evening Post*

Below: A popular film with a railway setting was David Lean's romantic 1949 blockbuster *Brief Encounter* starring Trevor Howard and Celia Johnson, which was filmed partly on location at Carnforth railway station. *Courtesy of Bob Gregson*

From brewery to cinema: the Picturedrome, Preston. Musical accompaniment featured live musicians and sometimes sound effects. The actors looked slightly inebriated while walking with a definite twitch, shake or tremble at an accelerated speed! *Lancashire Evening Post*

her first film, *Sally in our Alley* (1931), and gained increased popularity through films between 1936 and 1940. Playing women of humble origin working at the mill, she endeared herself to her audiences.

Iconic stars were now alternating between live performances and the new film medium, with the popular theatre audience captured and overtaken by the expansion of the talkies. In 1933 George Formby's first film, *Boots, Boots, Boots*, paved the way for acceptance by a much wider audience beyond the north/south divide. George was one of the highest-paid entertainers of the 1930s, and his natural broad Lancashire accent and cheerful disposition symbolised the working classes. People could readily identify with his large number of risqué songs and came to regard him as a gormless yet loveable Lancashire everyman. George made 21 films between 1934 and 1946.

In 1959 Sir Laurence Olivier epitomised the dying music hall era when he played the part of a struggling broken-down music hall comic in John Osborne's film *The Entertainer*, shot on location in Morecambe. The seedy Alhambra Theatre on the West End promenade was the perfect choice for the film company. The film also features interior shots of Morecambe Winter Gardens Theatre, which has since been restored.

The developing cinema industry was to have serious implications for the music hall industry. In the first decade of the 20th century the music hall held a mass appeal as impresarios and syndicate owners capitalised on the resurgent demand for that culture. But the so-called 'good old days' of the popular entertainment industry were being transformed from the music hall to the variety theatre, the former gradually moving away from being an essentially working-class form of entertainment towards having a mass appeal.

It was in the 1890s that that Moss, Thornton and Stoll began building many Empires, Palaces and Hippodromes throughout England, not only in London but also the provinces, continuing during the Edwardian era. There were more than 260 theatres open throughout Britain in 1901, illustrating the flourishing state of the theatrical industry; Liverpool had eight, while Manchester and Glasgow had seven apiece. They were the golden years of British music hall when all classes were attracted to the variety halls.

Theatre groups and their crews toured the provinces by rail as did renowned music hall performers. Two veterans of the music hall stage and film were the famous duo Laurel and Hardy, who starred in 107 films. At the height of their fame they were the most popular double act the world over, and were no strangers to Britain's variety theatres. They appeared on stage

Comedy duo Laurel and Hardy topped the bill at the Liverpool Empire theatre with their twice-nightly routine of slapstick comedy. Courtesy of Bob Gregson

The rise of cinema and decline of music hall

at the Liverpool Empire in 1947 and, after finishing their film career, they did a music hall tour of England and Scotland in the 1950s, appearing again at the Liverpool Empire during 1952 and 1953.

In 2019 the new biopic movie *Stan and Ollie* was launched starring Steve Coogan and John C. Reilly. Analysis of the credits showed location shots to be on the heritage Great Central Railway, Hackney Empire (masquerading as the London Lyceum) and the preserved ship MV *Balmoral*. This again highlighted how music hall stars travelled the country by the grand old steam-hauled trains of yesteryear.

During two World Wars the railways played a significant part in carrying music hall artists to comfort the troops. The First World War was probably the high-water mark of music hall popularity. Songs dealing with the war spoke mostly of the desire to return home: patriotic music hall compositions such as 'Keep the Home Fires Burning' and 'It's a Long Way to Tipperary' were sung by music hall audiences. Florrie Forde boosted morale with the rallying song 'Pack up Your Troubles in Your Old Kit Bag' when she appeared at Preston's Royal Hippodrome in October 1917.

As a distinct genre, variety was the most widespread form of urban entertainment throughout the Victorian and Edwardian eras, but thereafter began to absorb other entertainment styles, notably revue, musicals, jazz, swing, and big-band dance music acts. Apart from cinema, music hall had to compete with Entertainment Tax and a range of popular entertainments, especially sport and dancing, gramophone records and radio. The *Gramophone Review* of 1928 asked, 'Why, we ask ourselves, should we go out in cold and wet, into crowds, perhaps to see some entertainment that we cannot be sure of enjoying, when we have a comfortable chair and fifteen records of Rigoletto to entrance us?'

With the outbreak of the Second World War the free buffet on Preston railway station once again saw active service for members of His Majesty's Forces, and the local variety theatre had a funding part to play. Meanwhile the Nazi threats of bombings were bravely ignored by patrons in theatres throughout the country. Variety theatres provided an escape from the problems of the world at that time. Theatre programmes did, however, contain certain warnings, and this was no less applicable at the King's Palace, Preston, whose programmes warned patrons to 'Please bring your gas mask with you!'

This Christmas 1939 all-star variety programme at the King's Palace Theatre was to raise funds for Preston railway station's free buffet. *Author's collection*

Variety and revue predominated before, during and after the Second World War, though the ranges of performances at Preston's Royal Hippodrome were more diverse, especially when the distinguished actor John Mills starred in the play *A Duet for Two Hands* during 1945.

A resurgence of interest in variety during the 1940 and '50s was evident with comedy reflecting the culture of northern humour and exploited by numerous

northern comics. J. B. Priestley famously said in 1934: 'If you are a southerner, you may imagine that you have landed amongst a million music hall comedians.'

During the second quarter of the 20th century comedians, singers, ventriloquists and many more classic variety acts toured the halls of Britain extensively, most of them travelling by train. Passengers included Frank Randle, Hylda Baker and Cynthia, Jimmy Jewel and Ben Warriss, Norman Evans, Max Miller, Jimmy James, Eric Morecambe and Ernie Wise, Robb Wilton, Tommy Trinder, Albert Modley, Flanagan and Allen, the Crazy Gang, Arthur Worsley and Charlie Brown, Terry Hall and Lenny the Lion, Peter Brough and Archie Andrews, Keith Harris and Orville, Richard Tauber, Frankie Vaughan, G. H. Elliot, Tessie O'Shea, Shirley Bassey, Julie Andrews, and that real veteran of the music hall stage, Florrie Forde.

Musical comedy, revue and repertory prospered too, and repertory companies toured the provinces. However, the mid-20th century witnessed the permanent demise of the commercial variety theatre, attributed to the popularity of television and rising costs in all branches of the business. Changes in culture, television, ten pin bowling and trendy coffee bars took their toll. Many blows had struck live entertainment broadside throughout the 1950s, and this pattern continued unabated throughout Britain.

The largest British music hall chain, Moss Empires, closed several of its major variety theatres in the early 1960s when thousands of variety theatres throughout Britain saw the final curtain call during the 1950s and into the following decade. Many music hall performers, unable to find work, fell into poverty; some

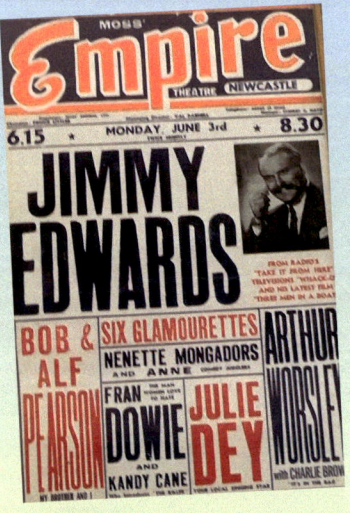

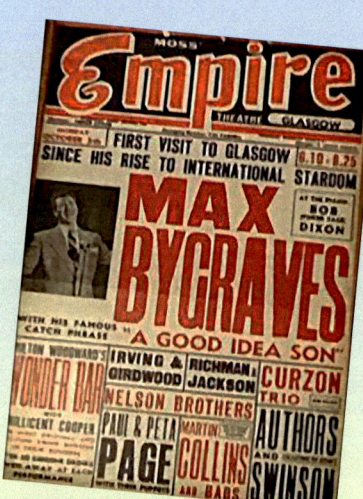

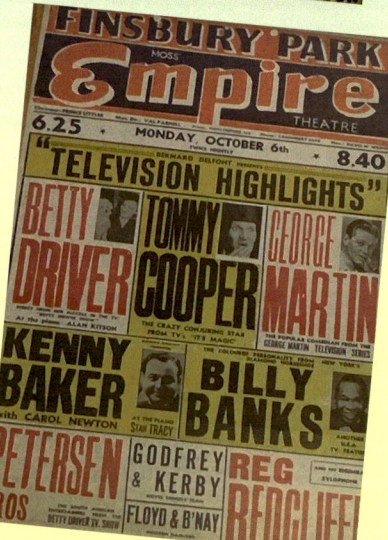

Variety acts were still extant at Moss Empire's theatres in the 1950s. Sadly, the Finsbury Park Empire, Newcastle Theatre Royal and Glasgow's notorious Empire are no more. Topping the bill at Newcastle was a young Bruce Forsyth on his way to stardom. *Courtesy of Kevin O'Connor, The Marine Lake Café, Southport*

The rise of cinema and decline of music hall

did not even have a home, having spent their working lives living in digs between performances.

At about this time John Osborne wrote that 'the music hall is dying and with it a significant part of England. Some of the heart of England has gone, something that belonged to everyone, for this is truly a folk art.'

In the 1950s, Bill Haley and His Comets and other rock and roll performers topped the variety theatre bills and attracted a young audience while driving the older audiences away. The advent of television and changes in culture such as this changed everything and spelled the end of the variety theatres.

Today variety as we knew it is dead and likely to remain so. One by one the magnificent baroque interiors have been bulldozed to the ground to make way for developments of another kind. Truly this is a far cry from the late Victorian and Edwardian eras, when music hall became such an integral part of the nation's social history.

The heyday of cinema in Britain was the two decades from 1930 to 1950. After the televising of the Coronation in 1953, the final nail in the coffin of town-centre cinemas was sealed, and their demise continued unabated until the resurgence of multi-screens in the 1960s.

Lancashire's forgotten music halls
Preston's three variety theatres of the 20th century, the Royal Hippodrome (1905), the Empire Theatre (1911) and the King's Palace (1913), were all opened during the town's golden years of variety. With the provision of live theatre at Preston's remodelled Theatre Royal (1802) and Gaiety Palace Theatre of Varieties Music Hall of 1882, Preston maintained a total of five live theatres during the first two decades of the 20th century. The city's

The final curtain: dancing girls are no more at the Royal Hippodrome, Preston. *Courtesy of the Lancashire Post*

two remaining variety theatres became more victims of the countrywide theatre closures during the 1950s; the King's Palace and the Royal Hippodrome brought down the final curtain on variety when they closed for good in February 1955 and May 1957 respectively.

The Preston model can be usefully compared with three other similarly sized former Lancashire towns, Accrington, Burnley and Blackburn, which each had at least one purpose-built music hall at the turn of the century.

At Blackburn (population 120,064 in 1891) two theatres had opened in the late 18th century. The earliest drama theatre was The Theatre Royal, Ainsworth Street, which had opened as early as 1775. It became the Theatre Royal and Opera House in 1818 with three entrances, a gallery and a pit. The theatre was reconstructed in 1886 and renovated in 1909, now offered luxury furnished saloons, a seating capacity for 1,687, standing room for 700, and yet another change of name to the Royal Hippodrome and Opera House.

The New Theatre opened in 1787 utilising the old Assembly Rooms in Market Street Lane. It successively became the Alhambra Palace, the Royalty and New Royalty Theatre. Its final incarnation was The Lyceum Theatre of Varieties, a music hall that closed in 1902 due to a problem with licensing.

The Prince's Theatre, Jubilee Street, Blackburn, opened in about 1890. It was renamed the Grand in December 1931 and closed as a variety theatre in 1956. Next door to the Grand Theatre, the Palace Music Hall fronting the Boulevard opened on 11 December 1899 'with a first-class variety bill'. It reopened as part of the McNaughten circuit in September 1900. The Palace catered for the working class, who took advantage of the largest 'gods' (the uppermost tier or gallery) in the county; it had a capacity of 1,000, with patrons paying the princely sum of tuppence a ticket. As a lesson to the rowdy elements of the audience, the manager on one occasion closed down the entire gallery. The last of the Blackburn music halls opened in 1911 as The Olympia. It was handsomely decorated with a mahogany foyer and entrance hall lit by eight flame arc lamps to welcome families and the more affluent members of Blackburn society.

Burnley had two drama theatres, the Victoria and the Gaiety. The continuity of Burnley's music hall industry in the 1890s is illustrated by the construction of its first purpose-built music hall, The Empire, which opened on 29 October 1894. It was designed by the architect G. B. Rawcliffe, who had previously designed the Victoria Opera House in Burnley. The theatre

The New Hippodrome Theatre, Accrington, opened in December 1908. In later years it followed a downward spiral of variety, revue and finally nude revues. It closed in 1955 and was demolished in the 1960s. *Courtesy of Bob Gregson*

The rise of cinema and decline of music hall

originally accommodated 1,935 people. In 1911 the respected theatre architect Bertie Crewe reconstructed the auditorium with a new seating capacity of 2,100. It is Crewe's auditorium that remains to this day, despite several changes of use and neglect over the last 20 years. The Empire was unchallenged as a variety theatre until 1908 when the Palace Hippodrome, having 2,000 seats, opened in the centre of town in December 1907.

In Lancashire's textile towns, the trend for music hall to adopt an image of respectability is illustrated by a speech given by Frank McNaughten at the opening of the Burnley Palace Hippodrome in 1908:

'I am often asked why I call my halls Palaces and Hippodromes. This is to draw a distinction between the old music hall of the past, frequented by men only, and the new Vaudeville entertainment of the present day, to be patronised by women and children… The old music hall is in the transition stage from the singing room to the new Vaudeville Variety theatre.'

At Barrow-in-Furness, Cumbria (formerly Lancashire), there was a wealth of cinemas to choose from: the Coliseum, Electric Theatre, Essoldo, Hippodrome, Pavilion, Ritz, Roxy, Royalty and the Tivoli Music Hall (formerly the Alexandra) on Forshaw Street, which opened in 1867. Her Majesty's Theatre was the last commercial theatre to close in the town in 1973.

Above: Preserved Furness Railway No 20 at Haverthwaite, with Victorian ladies in costume – perhaps bound for Barrow's Tivoli music hall? *Courtesy of Peter Fitton*

Left: Tramcars had an almost harmonious existence with music halls. *Courtesy of Bob Gregson*

All change for the Beatles in Lancashire

In the 1960s thousands of young people were to drool over a new generation of pop singers – legendary names such as Elvis Presley, Johnnie Ray, Lonnie Donegan and his skiffle group, Tommy Steele, Cliff Richard and, of course, the Beatles.

This spelled the end of the variety theatres. In 1957 a local pop group called the Quarrymen appeared at the Liverpool Empire theatre. They returned in 1959, having changed their name to Johnny and the Moondogs. They were back at the Empire again in 1962, now named the Beatles. Affectionately known by their fans as 'the Fab Four', they played the Empire for the last time on 5 December 1965.

On 26 October 1962 this obscure pop group from Liverpool was paid £18 to support Mike Berry and the Outlaws when appearing at the Public Hall, Preston, on the occasion of the annual Grasshopper Rugby Club Dance. Their first single, *From Me to You*, had just been released and tickets cost 6 shillings. They even returned to the Public Hall the following year on 13 September 1963 for another gig, but this time to wider acclaim.

The Beatles travelled around Lancashire extensively from 1961 to late 1964 performing at Fleetwood Marine Hall, Morecambe Floral Hall, Wigan, Nelson, and at Blackburn's King George's Hall on 9 June 1963, co-starring with Roy Orbison. They played more than 40 times in the county, and in 1963 alone appeared 23 times at various venues.

At Blackpool they topped the bill at the Queen's variety theatre, where they had to be lowered into the theatre through a trap door in the roof to avoid the screaming fans blocking the entrances. They were also top of the bill at the lavish ABC Theatre, Blackpool, now demolished, on 18 July 1964. A more usual haunt of the Beatles was Southport, where they appeared at the Southport Kingsway Club, as well as the Odeon Cinema, about 12 times between March 1961 and October 1963. In their native Liverpool they made several appearances at the Liverpool Empire – and the rest, as they say, is history.

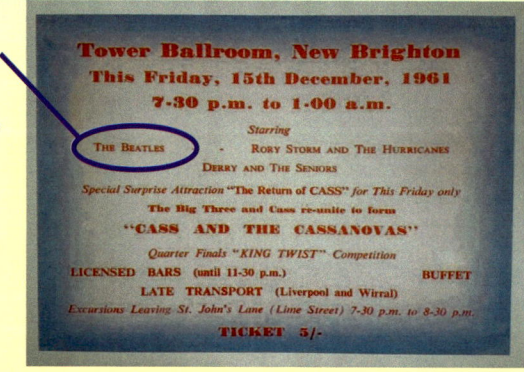

Right: A Christmas cracker with the Beatles at The Tower, New Brighton, in December 1961.

Far right: The Public Hall, Preston, formerly the Corn Exchange. Author

Chapter Nine – 'I do like to be beside the seaside'

One of the most popular songs of the music hall era was Florrie Forde's 'I do like to be beside the seaside', for the seaside has always been popular with holidaymakers. Where you found holidaymakers you would also have found concert parties, Punch and Judy shows, pierrot troupes, variety theatres, risqué postcards, seaside piers presenting summer shows and, of course, a rich assortment of steam-hauled trains.

As well as transporting performers, the railways also brought audiences in their thousands to Britain's seaside resorts to see the summer shows during the 'Wakes Weeks', which were a legacy of the Industrial Revolution and originally governed by the resilient textile industry. Many workers simply refused to turn in after a brief holiday, so mill owners closed factories to clean and service machines while thousands of employees enjoyed their annual holiday. Nowadays the wakes are in permanent slumber, the weaving sheds of Lancashire and Yorkshire are silent and not a single bobbin is left turning.

Courtesy of Bob Gregson

The annual Bass Brewery excursion to Blackpool in 1900. *Courtesy of Bob Gregson*

A Blackpool-bound train passes Ashton, Preston, in about 1920. *Courtesy of Bob Gregson*

Blackpool holidaymakers arrive at Blackpool. The variety and theatre industry thrived during the Wakes Weeks. *Courtesy of Bob Gregson*

At Burton-on-Trent the Bass Brewery began to offer its employees and their families a day out to the seaside by excursion train. By 1889 this had become a regular event with as many as 15 trains leaving Burton en route to the coast carrying up to 10,000 people eagerly anticipating their arrival. Imagine the logistical management involved. Sometimes there might be more than ten separate trains setting off at the same time from Burton to Liverpool or Scarborough.

In 1867 the Furness & Midland Joint Railway and the LNWR gave birth to Morecambe as a holiday resort for the many holidaymakers who travelled from West Yorkshire via Carnforth. The abundance of summer excursion traffic over the line from Leeds and Bradford in particular led to Morecambe being dubbed 'Bradford by the Sea'. This line, avoiding Lancaster, was originally conceived as

Class 'B1' No 61071 waits to leave Scarborough station. *Courtesy of Bob Gregson*

'I do like to be beside the seaside'

a joint venture between the Furness Railway and the Midland Railway.

At the turn of the 20th century Blackpool, Morecambe and coastal resorts along the Lancashire and Cumbrian coast abounded in white-faced pierrots and concert party companies performing in the open air or at the end of the pier. Daily orchestral music delighted visitors in the huge glass pavilion on Morecambe's West End Pier, while down below entertainers had performed on the sands since 1899. Morecambe sands near the Old Stone Jetty was the venue for Papa Parson's all-ladies troupe known as the Lucky Little Lancashire Lassies – in reality his wife and seven daughters. Could this have been a precursor to the Spice Girls?

Fifty years later visitors still had a wide choice of entertainment in the resort's cinemas and theatres, ranging from Henry Claxton's regular summer revue *Gaytime* at the Palace Theatre, Sandylands Promenade, to Eddie Morrell's *Starlights* in its 20th season at the long-gone Central Pier (built 1869). Morecambe Winter Gardens staged traditional music hall acts like the town's own Albert Modley, while the prominent Alhambra Theatre staged its sleazy summer revue.

Comic Norman Evans peers over the garden wall, advertising his Scarborough Floral Hall 1954 summer show. *Author's collection*

Electric multiple unit No 28220 at Lancaster bound for Morecambe; this line was electrified as early as 1908. *Courtesy of Bob Gregson*

Smile for the camera – holidaymakers arrive at Morecambe Promenade station. *Courtesy of Bob Gregson*

A rare programme: Florrie Ford recaptured the music hall atmosphere at Morecambe Winter Gardens as late as 30 August 1938. *Author's collection*

During the mid-1950s Morecambe Royalty Theatre, long associated with Thora Hird, was drifting towards closure as a live theatre. It had opened on 14th April 1898, with a capacity for 1,555 people both standing and sitting in stalls, circles and private boxes. It held theatre performances throughout the year and showed films during the winter season. It became a cinema in 1961, then a bingo hall before closing as a cinema again in 1967. It was demolished in 1972.

In 1897 the Victoria Pavilion, later Morecambe Winter Gardens Theatre, opened as a music hall on the site of a former entertainment complex that incorporated seawater baths, bars and a ballroom.

Florrie Forde (16 August 1875-18 April 1940) was an Australian popular singer and legendary music hall entertainer. From 1897 she lived and worked in the United Kingdom. Her legacy of music hall songs includes 'Has anyone here seen Kelly', 'She's a lassie from Lancashire', 'Hold your hand out, naughty boy', 'Down at the Old Bull and Bush', 'I do like to beside the seaside' and the rallying wartime songs 'Pack up your troubles' and 'It's a long way to Tipperary'. In the 1950s the Winter Gardens were taken over by Moss Empires, but the theatre was closed for long periods in winter and became unviable.

During the Swinging Sixties my wife Dorothy and I enjoyed an evening performance of *The Black and White Minstrel Show* at the Winter Gardens, following a grand tour of the Lake District on my Lambretta scooter. This was to be my only visit to that theatre before it closed for good in 1977, due to poor box office returns.

Fortunately, in 2006 Evelyn Archer and the Friends of the Winter Gardens formed the Morecambe Winter Gardens Preservation Trust, with a view to restoring the theatre to its former glory, hopefully with substantial grant and lottery funding. Significantly, in February 2006 the trust purchased the building, then in 2008, as part of an appraisal of the Morecambe Conservation Area, the Winter Gardens were listed as one of the area's most significant features, as the main example of the remnants of the resort's 19th-century entertainment buildings.

The ballroom building was demolished in 1982, though the theatre has been Grade II listed since closure. The Winter Gardens are unique and one of only a few surviving examples of a traditional large Victorian variety theatre, with a capacity of more than 2,000. It retains many original features, including marble steps leading

'I do like to be beside the seaside'

to a three-tiered auditorium with an old-style proscenium framed by ornate boxes. The stage has seen all the greats of music hall and variety as well as melodrama, musicals, revue and opera.

On 15 July 1840 the Preston & Wyre Railway opened, connecting Preston with Fleetwood and with ambitious plans for the development of Fleetwood as a port. Fleetwood was created by the railway. By the late 1840s those factory workers who wanted to 'be beside the seaside' could board a train from the cotton towns to Fleetwood with cheap Sunday excursions departing from Preston at 7.40am and arriving at Fleetwood at 9.00am.

It was not until February 1846 that a branch from Poulton-le-Fylde to Blackpool North established Blackpool as a popular seaside resort.

The Morecambe Bay paddle steamers plying between Fleetwood and Barrow brought holidaymakers to the Lake District and Fylde coast resorts. The voyage took nearly 2 hours and four ships made the crossing. Illustrated are the PS Lady Evelyn, introduced in 1900, and PS Lady Moyra of 1910.

The town developed in the late 19th century with a catchment area embracing Lancashire and Yorkshire's mill towns and other great centres of industry. From Oldham alone during 1860 more than 23,000 holidaymakers travelled on special trains to the resort.

By steam ship to the Music Halls

Offshore Blackpool and the Fylde was once adorned by paddle steamers that sailed from the piers. The Furness Railway ran a regular paddle steamer crossing between Barrow and

Fleetwood, which brought thousands of visitors to the resort to ascend the famous tower or perhaps see a show. During the bay crossing refreshments and entertainment were provided as well as an opportunity to be photographed by Barrow photographer Edward Sankey.

Numerous excursions packed with excited families flocked to Blackpool to catch an early glimpse of the newly constructed Blackpool Tower and the neighbouring 'Big Wheel'. Many of Blackpool's famous attractions were built in the latter half of the 19th century, including the North Pier (1863), Central Pier (1868), South Pier (1894) and the world-famous Blackpool Tower (1894). Blackpool was to emerge as a magical archetypal seaside resort by the mid-20th century; nowhere else in the country could such a cast of famous stars be found during the summer season. Blackpool boasted about 12 variety theatres during the 1950s offering star-studded entertainment with many great names of the past.

Blackpool and the 'Golden Mile' evoke memories of the famous tramway with its fleet of old-fashioned tramcars, as well as childhood pleasures: donkey rides, playing with buckets and spades and making sandcastles, rides on carousels and watching the Punch and Judy show, all this while relishing fish and chips, ice cream,

The LMS advertised the popular entertainment industry at Blackpool, especially its theatres and cinemas, as well as circus and a host of other entertainment venues. *Courtesy of Bob Gregson*

Blackpool Central station during the 1950s. *Courtesy of Bob Gregson*

candyfloss, and cockles and whelks, though not necessarily in that order or all at once!

There was the end of the pier show too, where comedian Frank Randle entertained with risqué jokes. The north/south divide was influenced by the ideologies of the archetypal northerner. Randle enjoyed a reputation as 'the bad boy of northern comedy', with massive success on stage and screen. Blackpool Watch Committee banned his show *Randles Scandals*, regarding it as obscene. In revenge Randle hired an aeroplane and dropped a load of toilet rolls onto the town.

The Hippodrome Theatre, Church

'I do like to be beside the seaside'

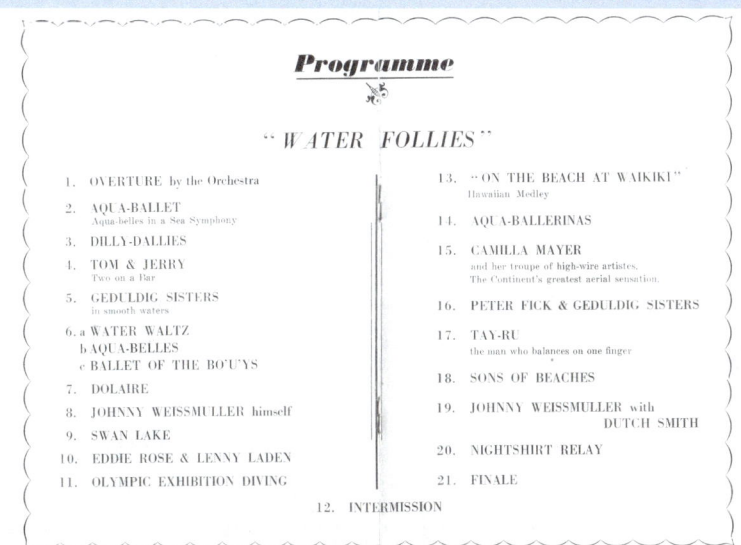

During the heyday of Blackpool's variety entertainment industry live shows were accommodated at the resort's Derby Baths. Even Johnny Weissmuller, famous as the screen's 'Tarzan', made a guest appearance here in 1949 in a 'Water Follies' spectacular. *Author*

Coach excursions at Blackpool were popular during the Wakes Weeks. *Courtesy of Leyland Transport Museum*

Street, Blackpool, was born at the time of the variety entertainment boom of the 1890s. It opened as the Empire Theatre of Varieties and was dubbed the 'largest theatre of varieties in the kingdom'. In 1900 it was renamed the Hippodrome and accordingly staged circus as well as variety. From the outset it was beset with problems and had a roller coaster existence with a string of owners and changes of name. In 1910 it reopened as a cinema with the added attraction of cine-variety. With the coming of the talkies the theatre was taken over by the expanding ABC circuit and the Hippodrome was the first cinema in the resort to project a talking movie, presented on 29 March 1929. *The Singing Fool* starred Al Jolson and caused a sensation; hundreds queued for every performance, and more than 60,000 saw the film in six weeks.

In 1948 a revue based on Hollywood's famous 'Coconut Grove' night spot was presented. It starred comedy duo Jewel and Warriss, singer Joseph Locke, some good speciality acts and showgirls who posed semi-nude in exotic sets. The show had a long and successful run and featured up and coming artists, in particular a young Julie Andrews.

From 1954 the Hippodrome presented conventional summer variety and revue, as well as the staging of the ITV sitcom *The Army Game*, 1960s pop stars and the musical *Rose Marie* in 1961, with David Whitfield. The theatre closed on Saturday 28 October 1961 with a showing of the film *Breakfast at Tiffany's*, starring Audrey Hepburn.

The ABC group rebuilt the ABC Theatre on the same site and many famous names appeared on stage, including Cliff Richard and the Beatles. The last summer shows ended in 1980 and the ABC became a full-time cinema. Unfortunately the theatre was to suffer the same fate as the Blackpool Hippodrome, closing in 2000 to become the Syndicate Nightclub in 2002. The venue was apparently not a big hit and the final act is that of a car park.

The Winter Gardens entertainment complex in Blackpool opened in 1875 and housed the Pavilion Theatre, which opened in 1878. It is a historic venue that formerly staged variety, revue and cinema from 1930. Sadly, since 1979 the Pavilion has no longer staged live shows. In the 1980s the theatre was partially converted, with the former stage becoming a café, though the Victorian auditorium remains as a legacy to Blackpool's variety entertainment industry.

In 1896 the Winter Gardens opened its own version of the 'London Eye' at the corner of Adelaide Street and Coronation Street. Unfortunately, the 220-feet-high wheel, with its 30 carriages holding 30 or more passengers, was never a great success and it made its last trip on 20 October 1928, and was demolished shortly afterwards.

Within the same complex the first Blackpool Opera House was built in 1889, at a cost of £9,098 and designed by Frank Matcham. It has since been rebuilt twice, in 1910 and 1939. The present theatre opened in 1939 as an art deco super theatre and cinema staging spectacular summer shows. With a capacity of 2,920, it is still

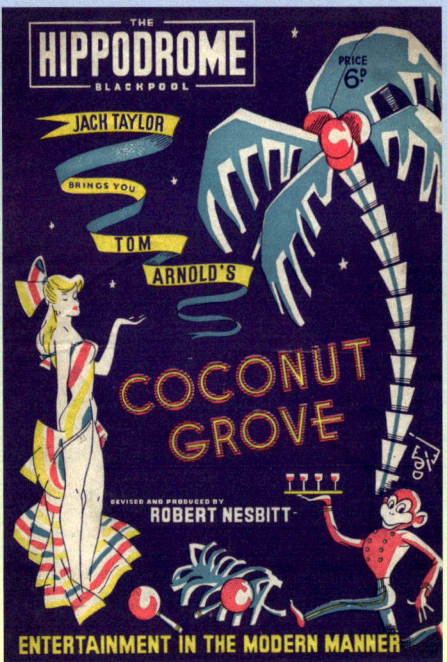

The programme for the 1949 revue 'Coconut Grove' at Blackpool Hippodrome; it starred comedy duo Jewel and Warriss and young Julie Andrews early in her musical career. *Author's collection*

'I do like to be beside the seaside'

Blackpool's Winter Gardens in circa 1900. To the right is the long-gone Ferris wheel, constructed in 1896. *Courtesy of Bob Gregson*

The summer show at Blackpool Opera House in 1958. *Author's collection*

one of the largest theatres in Britain. The theatre staged the Royal Variety Show in 2009 and nowadays tends to be opened intermittently with musicals and one-night performances.

In 1973 the Winter Gardens complex was granted a Grade II* listing, and is now owned by Blackpool Council, which purchased it in 2010.

The Queen's Theatre, Blackpool, originally opened as the Borough Theatre on 3 September 1877 with a production by the London Opera and Burlesque Company. The theatre seating 800, closed after only two years in 1879 and was renamed Bannisters Bazaar. It reopened as the Feldman's variety theatre in 1928 with touring variety and revues.

The theatre, constructed with two tiers and seating 1,000, was bought by Jimmy Brennan in 1951 and reopened in 1953 as the Queen's

The façade of the Winter Gardens in 2018. *Valerie Faheem*

the Pavilion, Liverpool, and the Hulme Hippodrome, which were all owned by Jimmy Brennan.

Blackpool Tower was designed by James Maxwell and Charles Tuke, from an original idea by Blackpool's Mayor, John Bickerstaff, inspired by Paris's Eiffel Tower; he invested £2,000 of his own money in the project. The total construction costs were £290,000 and both its architects died before completion. The menagerie of 'Albert and the Lion' notoriety, made famous by Stanley Holloway, closed in 1973, when the animals were transferred to the new Blackpool Zoo.

Frank Matcham excelled with the designs of both Blackpool Tower circus and ballroom, the latter opening in 1899. The famous ballroom was built for the Blackpool Tower Company as part of the seaside town's regeneration to attract tourism. The ballroom was seriously damaged in a fire in 1956, but was restored to its original design by Andrew Mazzei at a cost of £500,000 two years later. Both attractions happily survive within the Blackpool Tower complex.

Originally named the Alhambra Theatre, the Palace Theatre opened in 1899, next to the Tower, but closed in 1903. In July 1904 the Blackpool Tower Company reopened the theatre as the Palace of Varieties, presenting top twice-nightly variety shows 52 weeks a year. From 1956 to 1961 it presented summer

Theatre with a summer revue titled *Singing in the Reign* starring Josef Locke and Nat Jackley. A sign of the times, in the same year it was 'eyes down, look in' with bingo taking over from variety in winter. Nevertheless, Blackpool's heyday of variety and spectacular revues was still to the fore in the early 1950s and Jimmy Brennan put on a summer show each year for 16 weeks. The Queen's survived as a variety theatre until demolition in 1971. It was the end of an era too for the Wigan Hippodrome,

James Brennan's Queen's Theatre, Blackpool, presented revue and variety.

variety shows. The Palace complex comprised a cinema and ballroom as well as a variety theatre. The Palace building was demolished in 1962 to make way for a new John Lewis store, later to become a branch of Woolworth.

Consequently from 1875 until the mid-20th century Blackpool presented thriving recreational facilities at the Winter Gardens and Blackpool Tower complex, offering theatres, cinema, ballroom dancing, a menagerie and a circus, though several of these elements competed with the variety theatres.

Blackpool still has three piers, South, Central and North, all of which had theatres constructed on them. Only one theatre survives, on the North Pier; indeed, it is one of only five seaside piers in the country with a theatre staging variety. The North Pier is the oldest Blackpool pier, built in 1863, and is a Grade II listed building and the only Lancashire pier to hold that status. The pier theatre has hosted many famous stars including Frankie Vaughan, Bruce Forsyth, Des O'Connor, Frank Randle, Tessie O'Shea and Morecambe and Wise. to name but a few.

Left: The jewel in Blackpool's crown reaches 158 metres (500 feet) skywards above the resort.
Courtesy of Valerie Faheem

Right: The programme for *Secombe Here!* (1960). The Palace theatre, cinema and ballroom complex was the first of Blackpool's major theatres to close.

The Central Pier was built in 1868 and its Pavilion theatre fronted the promenade until the mid-1960s, when it was rebuilt as an amusement arcade. Variety entertainment switched to the end of the pier, which became a cabaret bar and is now a pub.

The South Pier opened in 1893 and is now home to 'white knuckle' rides, although its former theatres have had a chequered history. The Grand Pavilion was finally destroyed by a fire in 1964, being replaced by the Pier Head Theatre, which was superseded by a fairground in 1998, such is the way

Above: 'Strolling, just strolling' on the North Pier, Blackpool.
Courtesy of Bob Gregson

Left: The present North Pier Theatre opened in 1939 with a capacity for 1,564 people.
Courtesy of Valerie Faheem

Right: The North Pier Theatre auditorium in the summer of 2018.
Courtesy of Valerie Faheem

'I do like to be beside the seaside'

Left: A summer audience at the Central Pier heard comedian Al Read's famous catchphrase, 'Right, Monkey!' Author's collection

Right: The Victorian Grand Theatre, Blackpool, in 2018. Valerie Faheem

Below right and overleaf: Four excerpts from Blackpool's Comedy Carpet. Courtesy of Gordon Young and Why Not Associates, London

of commercial enterprise.

Despite the loss of so many theatres in Blackpool, the Opera House, North Pier Theatre and the stunning Grand Theatre remain as a legacy of an era lost in the mists of time. The Grand is the only theatre in Blackpool to open all year; having opened as a playhouse, it today presents plays, musicals, revue, pantomime and occasional recreated music hall. Moreover, that doyen of variety, Ken Dodd, regularly played the Grand on Sunday evenings up to 2017.

Today Blackpool's urban fabric and economy remain firmly rooted in the tourism sector. The promenade and sands continue to attract millions of visitors every year. Indeed, here there is an opportunity to wallow in the great names of the past on the Comedy Carpet fronting the iconic Blackpool Tower.

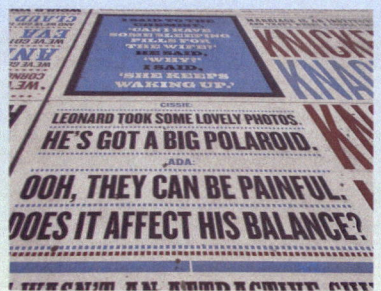

'Your programme, sir, for your delectation and delight'

Theatre programmes are a primary source of social history. Contemporary advertising also provides an insight into the commercial life of seaside resorts, towns and cities during the first half of the 20th century.

Over the years I have amassed a comprehensive collection featuring legendary artists. In the 1960s prices ranged from threepence to sixpence, a far cry from today's prices, as are the costs of theatre seats to enjoy a seaside show.

An October 1949 variety programme for Feldmans Theatre, later to be renamed The Queens. *Author's collection*

Right: A summer show at Blackpool Winter Gardens Pavilion starring Tommy Cooper. *Author's collection*

'I do like to be beside the seaside'

Right: A summer revue at the New Blackpool Opera House in 1949. Author's collection

Far right top: Harry Secombe and Harry Worth played the Blackpool Palace Summer Season in 1960. Author's collection

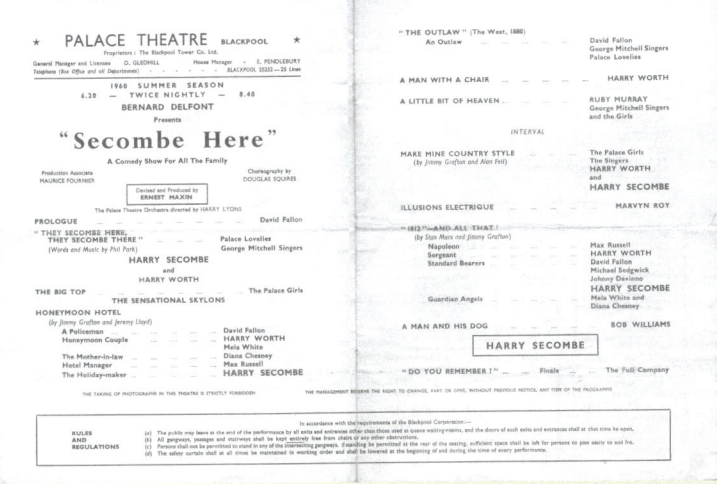

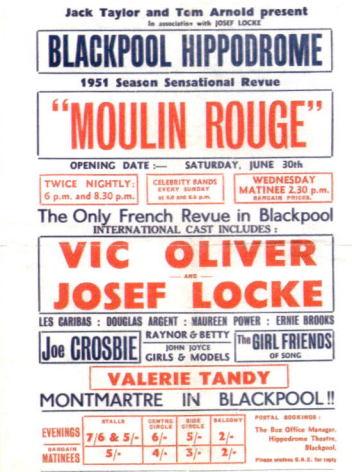

Left: The 1951 season's sensational revue 'Moulin Rouge' at the Blackpool Hippodrome – and all this for 7s 6d for the best seats in the stalls. Author's collection

Right: Dave Morris regularly played the Regal Theatre on Blackpool's South Pier. Author's collection

Ken Dodd made his debut in Blackpool in 1955, at the Central Pier, when he starred with Morecambe and Wise who were topping the bill in the variety show 'Let's Have Fun'. In 1956 he again appeared in 'Let's Have Fun' with Jimmy James, Roy Castle and Our Eli, and Jimmy Clitheroe here shown presenting their famous 'Box Routine'. *Author's collection*

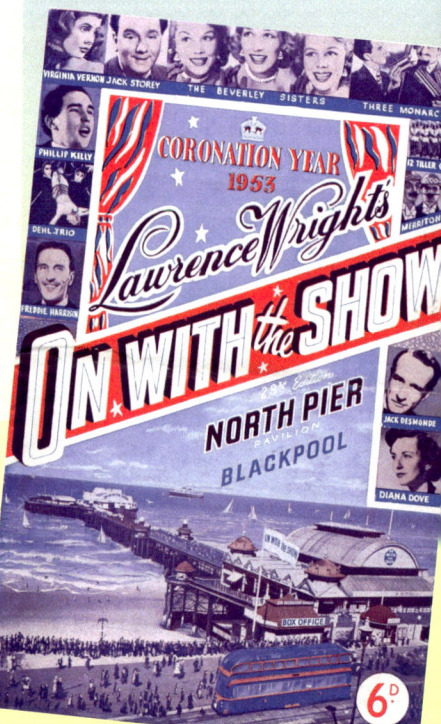

Stars of yesteryear appeared at the North Pier Pavilion during Coronation Year, 1953. *Author's collection*

Interval: A gallery of steam trains

'Ladies and gentlemen, we now take a 20th-century sentimental journey with a nostalgic look back at steam-hauled suburban, express and excursion trains, which conveyed audiences and performers to the variety theatres in the first half of the century. So sit back and enjoy the following pictures, all thanks to the photographic artistry of Stanley Withers Esquire.'

Preserved 'V2' No 4771 (BR No 60800) *Green Arrow* climbs Miles Platting bank after departing from Manchester Victoria with 1Z36, a charter working heading for York then London King's Cross, on 26 April 1986.

Above: BR Standard Class 4 4-6-0 No 75050 heads south at Lostock Hall with a Preston to Liverpool Exchange local service.

Above right: 'Jubilee' Class No 45590 *Travancore* departs from Leyland with an afternoon Preston to Wigan North Western stopping train in the mid-1960s.

Right: Stanier Class 5 No 45321 is seen at Farington Curve Junction with a Glasgow to Liverpool Exchange service circa 1964.

A gallery of steam trains

Above: Now preserved, ex-GWR 'Manor' Class No 7820 *Dinmore Manor* departs from Oswestry with a local service to Whitchurch in May 1963.

Above right: Fairburn tank No 42285 stands at Wakefield Westgate with the Bradford portion of a King's Cross to Leeds service in the early 1960s.

Right: Stanier Class 5 No 45227 waits at Leeds City station with the 15.35 service to Morecambe in July 1966.

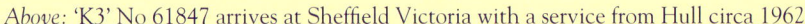

Above: 'K3' No 61847 arrives at Sheffield Victoria with a service from Hull circa 1962.

Above right: 'Flying Pig' No 43047 is seen at Manchester Central just before closure with one of the last steam services, the 12.48 service to Cheadle Heath.

Right: 'Crab' 2-6-0 No 47777 heads a Blackpool to Manchester Victoria service at Bolton Trinity Street in the mid-1960s.

A gallery of steam trains

Below: 'West Country' Class No 34097 *Holsworthy* approaches Vauxhall station with a Waterloo to Southampton service during July 1964.

Bottom: BR Standard No 73111 *King Uther* is also seen at Vauxhall with a Waterloo to Portsmouth service in July 1964.

Above: 'B1' Class No 61014 *Oribi* passes under Bee Lane Bridge, Farington Curve Junction, with a Liverpool Exchange to Glasgow train in the mid-1960s.

Insets: The signalman and the driver are keeping a look out and no doubt the lone trainspotter sitting on the retaining wall will have been noted by them! It is highly likely that the young lad has just underlined No 61014 *Oribi* in his Ian Allan ABC.

Above left: Another view at Vauxhall in July 1964, this time with 'Merchant Navy' Class No 35027 *Port Line* with the 'Bournemouth Belle' Pullman service.

Left: 'B1' Class No 61194 from Canklow heads an excursion from the Sheffield area in the mid-1960s.

Above: BR Standard No 73049 runs into Bath Green Park station with a Somerset & Dorset line train from Templecombe in July 1961.

A gallery of steam trains

Above left: GWR 0-6-0 pannier tank No 3742 runs light past Bath Green Park shed in July 1961.

Left: 'Royal Scot' No 46117 *Welsh Guardsman* passes Lostock Hall Station signal box with a Leeds to Blackpool excursion in early 1960.

Above: Nos 45109 and 75061 depart from the East Lancs side of Preston station with a Blackpool to Liverpool Exchange service in early 1960.

Right: 'Britannia' 'Pacific' No 70033 *Charles Dickens* passes Farington Goods Yard with a southbound express circa 1965.

Main picture: BR Standard No 75046 departs from Lostock Hall with a Liverpool Exchange to Blackpool service in about 1964.

A gallery of steam trains

Above left: Some time in the mid-1960s 'Britannia' Class No 70012 *John of Gaunt* waits for the signals in gloomy Manchester Victoria after arriving with a Blackpool service.

Above: Stanier Class 5 No 44800 attracts attention at Chester General station at the head of a parcels working on 5 March 1967.

Left: The driver of 'Jubilee' Class No 45710 *Irresistible* opens the cylinder cocks before departing from Manchester Victoria with a Euston to Colne service circa 1962.

Chapter Ten – 'All stations to Southport for a night out at the Garrick'

In this chapter I describe the origins and route of the former Preston to Southport branch line, which closed in September 1964. I also describe a visit to Southport's leading variety theatre of the 1950s period, the Garrick Theatre. Fortunately we can rekindle memories of the branch with an excellent photographic portfolio, kindly provided by my good friend, the late Alan Castle, unless credited otherwise.

The beginning of the Preston to Southport line

The last major railway construction project in the Preston area was the West Lancashire Railway (WLR) line from Fishergate Hill, Preston, to Southport via Hesketh Bank, opening on 15 September 1882 in time for that year's Guild celebrations.

Work had commenced on the 16-mile route from Preston to Southport on 19 April 1873. The WLR bridge spanning the River Ribble at Lower Penwortham (built alongside the old Broadgate road bridge) linked the WLR to the old terminus at Fishergate Hill, Preston. When completed it was tested with four locomotives running back and forth over it and not one fell in the river!

Stanier Class 5 No 44745 approaches Cop Lane. The principal cuttings along the branch, especially this one at Penwortham, were excavated using an American 'steam navvy'. This was the first machine of its kind to be used in railway construction and was capable of scooping out earth at the rate of 1,500 cubic yards every 24 hours.

The WLR was born at the end of a period of national railway construction and was integrated into the emergent rail network. Construction of the new line was intended to break the monopoly of the Lancashire & Yorkshire Railway (LYR) by providing a direct route as an alternative to the longer one from Southport via Burscough.

The section from Hesketh Bank to Penwortham presented engineering difficulties, in particular the crossing of the River Douglas at Hesketh Bank. The Douglas, a tributary of the Ribble, was crossed by a swing bridge to facilitate river navigation. Alongside the swing bridge was a halt that, although opened in 1882, closed after only five years; it had been intended for shipping and boat traffic sailing the River Douglas. One such vessel, a paddle steamer, named *The Virginia*, was owned by the WLR and was used to tow schooners up the Ribble to Preston Docks. It was the demise of this and other vessels during the late Victorian era that led to the Douglas bridge being permanently fixed.

The directors of the WLR at various times made plans to integrate their railway into several other grandiose railway projects. During 1882 management devised an ambitious proposal for a connecting line to Blackpool, leading from Hesketh Bank by way of a lengthy and costly viaduct across the Ribble to a point close to Freckleton Naze. However, the proposed bill was withdrawn following opposition from Preston Corporation, which wanted to improve the river for navigation purposes for the proposed Preston Dock.

The Hesketh Bank railway bridge completed the 16-mile railway route from Southport to Preston, which had taken a decade to construct. The line officially opened from Southport to the terminus at Fishergate Hill, Preston, in September 1882. At the time of the opening two 0-4-2 tender engines, manufactured by Sharp, Stewart

Above right: Hesketh Bank and the River Douglas bridge opening in 1899.

Right: Hesketh Bank station staff in 1899.

and Co of Manchester, were appropriately renamed *Southport* and *Longton*. A third engine named *Banks* was later delivered by the same firm in 1878.

The connection between the WLR and the LYR, near Preston, formed a triangular junction, known as Penwortham Triangle. The link opened for passengers in May 1883, and enabled trains to run direct between Southport and Blackburn.

However, construction of the completed line from Southport to Preston at Fishergate Hill led to the WLR being declared bankrupt, and in 1897 the company was absorbed by the LYR. The original terminus at Fishergate Hill was closed to passengers in 1900, after only 18 years. The surviving remnant of the original WLR saw occasional passenger use, when it played host to special services during several Preston Guilds.

The LYR had been incorporated in 1847 from an amalgamation of several existing railways based in northern England. It was not until 1850, however, that it gained a direct independent route into Preston from Bamber Bridge to the Butler Street terminus via Preston Junction and Whitehouse Junction.

This involved construction of a spectacular 52-arch bridge spanning the River Ribble between Avenham and Miller Parks, Preston. By 1883 sections of the viaduct were found to be structurally unsafe, and a costly operation was put into effect by filling in the arches and creating an embankment with earth, clay, rubble and refuse from landfill sites. Excavated material from the newly completed engine shed at Lostock Hall was also used to create the embankment. The iron bridge spanning the Ribble remains, though the arches have long since disappeared under the aforesaid embankment.

The Southport to Preston line was a forerunner of the electrification of the national railway network. From 22 March 1904 the line from Crossens to Southport was electrified using the third rail system, and from 15 February 1909 electrification was extended to Meols Cop.

Following complete closure of the Southport line in September 1964 the tracks were lifted during 1965, as was the goods-only line leading to the distinctive

A Preston to Southport train negotiates the curve at Whitehouse West Junction.

Demolition of the Ribble bridge at Broadgate, Preston.

Penwortham Cop Lane station was primitive, without gas or electricity, and comprised two small waiting rooms and a booking office, lit by paraffin lamps.

Fishergate Hill station. This station has since been demolished and only the piers of the old railway bridge alongside Penwortham old bridge remain as a legacy of the original course of the railway that once ran from Preston to Southport.

Memories of the Southport line

All the following photographs are courtesy of Alan Castle unless credited otherwise.

'The train now standing at Platform 12 is for all stations to Southport. This train will call at Penwortham Cop Lane, New Longton a& Hutton, Longton Bridge, Hoole, Hesketh Bank, Hundred End,

BR Standard No 78041 approaches Back Lane crossing. The next station west along the line was New Longton & Hutton.

Left: Fairburn tank No 42626 heads an up Preston-bound train at New Longton & Hutton station.

Below left: On 2 March 1963 Lostock Hall's Fairburn tank No 42154 heads the 1.02pm stopping train from Preston to Southport at Longton Bridge. *Peter Fitton*

Below: A rare visitor to the Southport branch was this Preston-bound 'Jubilee' Class steam-hauled train, seen leaving Hoole station.

Typical station architecture along the branch at Hesketh Bank, Crossens and Meols Cop stations. Electric trains ran between Southport and Crossens, and one is seen here at Meols Cop (*right*).

Banks, Crossens, Churchtown, Hesketh Park, St Lukes and Southport Chapel Street.'

To this day the sequence of station names and the journey itself, often behind a Fairburn 2-6-4 tank or Stanier Class 5 4-6-0 engine, are firmly lodged in my psyche. Although only 16 miles long, the line was dubbed the 'never never line' owing to the fact that with all those stations one never seemed to be getting any nearer to the end of the line at Southport Chapel Street!

I remember the Preston to Southport line not least for its quaint, innumerable country stations that ultimately led me to the south-west Lancashire seaside resort of Southport. The Southport branch symbolised the rural branch line before Beeching. Stations along the line had goods sheds, coal yards, timber crossings, quaint signal boxes, semaphore signals and cheery staff. There was little or no electric power and the buildings were for the most part illuminated by either gas or oil lanterns right up to the end. As was to be expected on such a rural line, the station buildings were small and typically boasted an attractive style of red-brick architecture.

The first station out of Preston was Penwortham Cop Lane, a simple halt built by the LYR in 1911. Up to 1940 the station

was simply called Cop Lane Halt before adopting its longer name.

Hundred End station provided a music hall joke on account of the farming industry it served, and was known by the locals as Celery Junction. On several occasions I recall being the only passenger to alight there, to go birdwatching on the remote Ribble marshes. This rural outpost was the first station along the branch to close, in 1962, heralding complete closure of the line two years later.

On the final approach to Southport an opportunity arose for an impromptu bout of trainspotting and I was surprised to see both green electric multiple units and a noteworthy steam locomotive. Southport station was the haunt of one of the last ex-LYR Aspinall Class 2P 2-4-2T tank locomotives, No 50781. I looked out for the locomotive performing its swansong duties, either shunting in the goods yard or acting as station pilot. It was a legacy of the LYR and was no stranger to the Southport branch.

Enjoying Southport with a visit to the theatre

On arrival at Southport there was the opportunity to visit the pleasure ground and take a ride on the big dipper, go out to sea in an ex wartime amphibious craft, or enjoy a leisurely stroll along the exceptionally long pier.

During the 1950s the seaside entertainment industry continued to prosper with veterans of the music hall stage playing the Garrick Theatre on Lord Street. This theatre, designed by local architect George Tonge in the Renaissance style, was built on the site of the Southport Opera House, part of the complex of the Southport Winter Gardens. The Opera House was another example of Frank Matcham's work, built near the old Cheshire Lines terminus on Lord Street. It was opened on 7 September 1891 and destroyed by fire in 1929.

On the Garrick Theatre's opening night, 19 December 1932, the curtain rose to a fanfare of trumpets. The first presentation was a mystery play, *Firebird*, which came direct from London's West End.

'All stations to Southport for a night out at the Garrick'

A lament for a variety theatre and railway branch line

Throughout its 25-year lifespan as a variety theatre the Garrick presented summer variety shows, musical comedies, drama and, of course, a Christmas pantomime. A combination of changing tastes and the opportunities for Britons to travel overseas on package holidays to the Mediterranean displaced the Lancashire seaside resorts as holiday destinations. Unfortunately, there was nothing to sustain either the ailing fortunes of the Preston to Southport branch or the Garrick Theatre, and the last major variety theatre in the resort closed in January 1957.

The new owners of the Garrick, the Essoldo Cinema Group, converted the building into a cinema and on 21 January 1957 the first double bill featured Elvis Presley in *Love Me Tender* and Maureen O'Hara in *Miracle on 34th Street*. There being no miracle to sustain the cinema's viability, it closed on 16 November 1963 with a final screening of *Tom Jones* starring Albert Finney.

Full-time bingo sessions were introduced in the 1970s, and in 1984 the premises were

Matcham's old Opera House, Southport, which was handy for the old Cheshire Lines railway station in Lord Street.

Right: Variety at the Garrick Theatre, Southport. George Formby is topping the variety bill; he regularly played Lancashire's music halls and seaside theatres.

Centre right: The Garrick Theatre is nicely portrayed on this programme, where Frank Randle starred in Randle's Scandals in 1950. Author's collection

Far right: There was also the Southport Pier Pavilion, the venue for this Christmas panto in December 1966. Author's collection

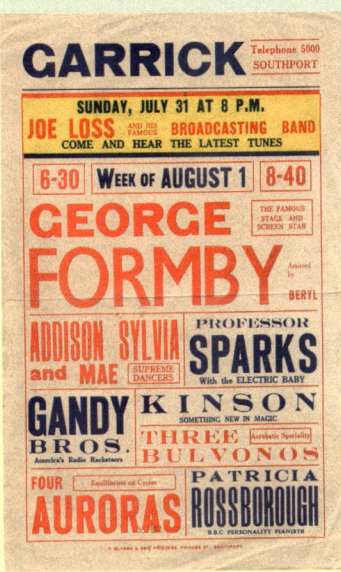
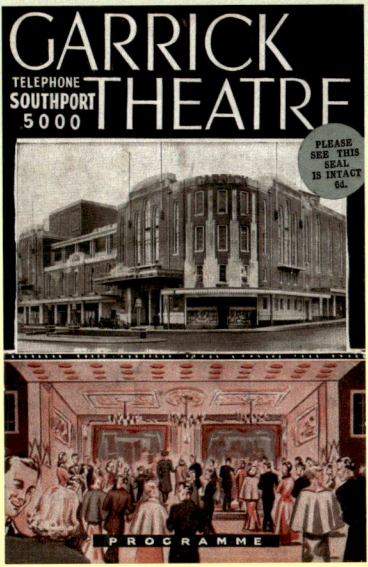
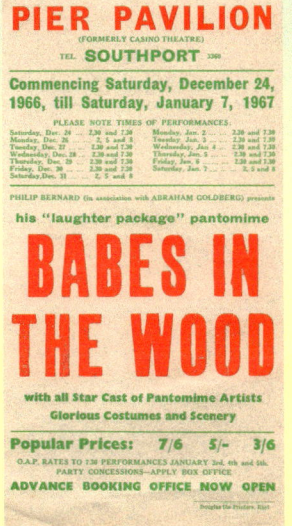

purchased by the Rank Organisation, which has operated the venue under the name of Mecca Bingo since 1997.

The Garrick Theatre originally had a capacity of 1,600, and today four boxes on two levels (stalls and circle) on either side of the 50-foot-wide proscenium belie its current use as a bingo hall. The theatre was Grade II listed in 1999, and although it is in excellent condition the hall has been levelled in the stalls area. A bar and buffet now occupy the stage area, where George Formby and a host of music hall stars once performed. The backstage areas and dressing rooms have been preserved, just in case it should ever revert to use as a live theatre.

A few years after the final curtain at the Garrick Theatre the branch line from

'All stations to Southport for a night out at the Garrick'

'Beeching axe'. This was wielded with the departure of the last passenger train to depart from Preston at 10.35pm on Sunday 6 September 1964. After 82 years of service the line was no more and the steam locomotive hauling the last train was appropriately daubed with a headboard bearing the words '1882-1964 Last Day'. The last electric train had run from Southport to Crossens on the preceding evening.

Not au revoir but goodbye to the Southport branch. The last trains left Southport Chapel Street station (*left*) and Preston station (*above and right*) on Sunday 6 September, 1964. Alan Castle prepared the special commemorative headboard carried by BR Standard locomotive No 78041.

Preston to Southport shared the same fate – closure. Alas, the era of both the seaside theatre and the rural branch line was about to hit the buffers for good.

In 1962 a certain Dr Richard Beeching recommended that more than 2,300 stations be closed, together with 18,000 miles of track. Sadly, the Preston to Southport branch line had always served a thinly populated rural district, and was an obvious candidate for the infamous

Chapter Eleven – By ship, steam train and horse-drawn tram to the Gaiety Theatre, Isle of Man

The Lady of Man leaving Fleetwood for Douglas. *Courtesy of Bob Gregson*

The Isle of Man Steam Packet Company is the oldest continually operating passenger shipping company in the world, having begun operations in 1830. Prior to that, the Isle of Man's population grew from 1767 when the first regular sailings started making the crossing of the Irish Sea.

During the Great War, 11 out of a total of 15 steam packet company vessels were requisitioned by the Admiralty; four were lost, three were retained by the Government, and four returned to service some four years later. During the Second World War Dunkirk was perhaps the company's finest hour, with *Mona's Isle* being the first vessel to leave Dover for Dunkirk and the first to complete the round trip during the evacuation. Eight company ships took part in the historic mission, rescuing a grand total of 24,699 British troops. The company has owned 72 vessels in total from its inception to the present day.

I was one of those not-so-old sea lags who boarded the SS *Viking* in 1952 and had to endure a force 10 gale during the crossing of the Irish Sea from Douglas to Fleetwood. The elegant twin-funnel vessel was the last coal-burning steamer in the steam packet fleet and went to the breaker's yard in 1954. Today passengers can still take a leisurely cruise across the Irish Sea, on *Ben-my-Chree*, which operates a conventional ferry service between Heysham and Douglas. From the open deck there is also a chance of spotting a variety of sea birds. With luck this might include Manx shearwaters, great skuas, kittiwakes, fulmars, gannets and guillemots, as well as rarer species.

By steam-hauled train to the Gaiety Theatre

Visitors flocked to the Isle of Man from the 1830s. The opening of the steam railway from 1873 to 1879 enabled resorts outside Douglas to flourish. The Isle of Man Railway's first line, from Douglas to Peel, was opened on 1 July 1873. The Port Erin line from Douglas, opened on 1 August 1874, 15½ miles long, is the last remaining section of the former 46-mile network. A third line was built in 1878-79 by a separate company, the Manx Northern Railway, and ran from St John's to Ramsey. Another short line was built from St John's to Foxdale in 1885 to serve the lead mines there.

The first trains to leave Ramsey, Peel and Port Erin were timed to arrive at Douglas at 8.00am to be in time for the morning ferries to the mainland. The next trains would leave Douglas, Peel, Port Erin and Ramsey around 10.00am, and there were also evening trains on all three main routes, but these quickly stopped during the Second World War.

In the 1930s, following the integration of train and bus services, it was usual for the summer train service to peak at about a dozen trains each way on all three main routes, and on an entirely single-track system. Although the railway was still intensively used in the summer time, by the mid-1950s winter train services had been reduced to morning and afternoon round trips to Port Erin and Peel, and a solitary working to Ramsey. These trains operated mainly for parcels traffic.

Sadly, passenger numbers continued to decrease while costs were increasing and this led to a progressive rundown of the system. Both the Peel and the Ramsey lines shut following the 1968 season, and in 1975 both lines were lifted; the Douglas to Port Erin line is all that remains.

All but one of the railway's distinctive locomotives were built by Beyer, Peacock & Company of Manchester between 1873 and 1926, with 16 steam locomotives in total. As of September 2015 there were nominally four locomotives in traffic, these being No 8 *Fenella*, No 10 *G. H. Wood*,

Two IOM steam trains pause at Ballasalla. *Courtesy of Richard Slee, 'Visit Isle of Man'*

A Victorian steam train traverses the idyllic countryside of the Isle of Man. *Courtesy of Richard Slee, 'Visit Isle of Man'*

No 12 *Hutchinson* and No 13 *Kissack*, and all contribute to a wonderful transport experience.

'Clickety-clop, clickety-clop': the Douglas horse-drawn trams

Before the age of the automobile and the omnibus islanders intending to see shows at the Gaiety Theatre would have taken the steam train or the Manx Electric Railway to Douglas, then the horse-drawn trams. This is the world's oldest surviving horse-drawn tram service, dating back to 1876. The trams are fitted with roller bearings to ease the load on the horses bred to pull them. The trams traverse the 2 miles from the Manx Electric Railway station and depot at Derby Castle along Douglas promenade to the sea terminal.

The tramway was built and initially operated by Thomas Lightfoot, a retired civil engineer from Sheffield. From its opening it has operated every year, except for a period during the Second World War, and since 1927 has run in the summer only. It is 3-foot gauge (914mm) and double track throughout, running down the middle of the road. Service is provided by 23 tramcars and some 45 lovely horses, known locally as 'trammers'. There have been several types of tramcar, and at least one of each type has been retained. During winter the trams are stored in a purpose-built tram shed.

In the summer of 2018 I travelled behind one of the 29 shire and Clydesdale horses that currently operate the service. I was surprised to see the conductor clinging precariously to the side of the tram while collecting fares. I was also intrigued to see him running alongside the tram, and giving it a shove to help the horse gain momentum, just like they did in the Victorian era.

It was nice to see and hear the equine quadrupeds that go with such a resonant clickety-clop along the promenade and good to know that in winter they have a well-earned rest.

The Gaiety Theatre: a Frank Matcham masterpiece

In 1893 the Pavilion Theatre was built on Douglas promenade at the height of the island's tourism boom. However, the venture was not a success, and the Pavilion closed after only six seasons.

Above: A choice of destinations on the Isle of Man Railway.

Right: A horse-drawn tram is about to commence a special return journey to Douglas Promenade. *Courtesy of Richard Slee, 'Visit Isle of Man'*

The Gaiety Theatre's fabulous auditorium.
Courtesy of Richard Slee, 'Visit Isle of Man'

The exterior of the Victorian Gaiety Theatre is equally impressive.
Courtesy of Richard Slee, 'Visit Isle of Man'

The new owners enlisted the services of Frank Matcham to carry out an extensive renovation of the theatre and his plans were presented to Douglas Corporation in March 1899. Part of the plans saw the creation of a glass ceiling in order to afford maximum light. The stage was extended and the resulting loss of seating was made up for by enlarging the circle and adding a third level. The new entrance facade, with its upstairs terrace and flamboyant decoration, took its inspiration from the buildings of the Italian Renaissance. The interior, with its ceiling paintings and ornate plasterwork, combined baroque and Elizabethan elements.

The theatre opened on 16 July 1900 with a West End production of *The Telephone Girl*. It enjoyed considerable success until the outbreak of the First World War, then after the war it fell into decline together with the island's tourist industry. Various attempts were made to regain its former commercial success with the installation of cinema equipment in the 1920s, but with the decline of the island's tourist industry by 1970 the theatre was just a signature away from demolition.

Fortunately, in 1971 the Isle of Man Government acquired the dilapidated building from the Palace and Derby Castle Company for the sum of £41,000 and carried out essential repairs and, in 1976, a programme of restoration. The theatre underwent further restoration in the 1990s to replicate its 1900 opening condition in time for the centenary celebration in 2000. Exactly 100 years after opening, on 16 July 2000, the centenary was celebrated with a performance of *The Telephone Girl*, which had opened the Gaiety in 1900.

The restoration of the Gaiety Theatre was directed over several years by the theatre manager of the day, Mervin Russell Stokes, who was later awarded an MBE for his contribution to the project. Mr Stokes worked with a view to strict authenticity, even down to having the original paint colours, wallpaper and carpeting recreated, together with the restoration of the Gaiety's famous 'Corsican Trap' and other period stage machinery.

Today the theatre continues with productions by local companies and touring productions of musicals, drama and opera. The Gaiety has seating for up to 800 people on three levels, with opulent boxes adding the finishing touches to the original auditorium.

Chapter Twelve – Nine great British music halls and variety theatres

'Twice nightly' – so said the music halls and variety theatres throughout Britain. In the days when the average weekly wage was £2, families had the opportunity to enjoy a pleasant night out together and still have some money left for fish and chips, a bag of scraps and a bottle of pop after the show. This was a time when families had the opportunity to have a pleasant night out, put on their best clothes and meet their friends. Music hall visits were social events attended by the family, friends and work colleagues.

'Ladies and gentlemen, by way of a special treat we proudly present for your delight and delectation a splendid portfolio of music halls and variety theatres. We begin with the oldest surviving music hall in London. Maestro, raise your baton, for we proudly present a cornucopia of captivating conviviality, packed with song and dance, novelty acts, special guest turns, side-splitting banter, and audience participation for your sincere unmitigated enjoyment.'

Wilton's Music Hall

Wilton's Music Hall is a Grade II* listed building and one of very few examples of a surviving mid-19th-century music hall, retaining many original features and a mesmerising history.

Originally an alehouse dating from 1743 or earlier, it may well have served the Scandinavian sea captains and wealthy merchants who lived in neighbouring Wellclose Square. In 1839 a concert room was built behind the pub and in 1843 it was licensed for a short time as the Albion Saloon, presenting full-length plays. John Wilton bought the business in about 1850, enlarged the concert room three years later, and replaced it with his 'Magnificent New Music Hall' in 1858.

Wilton's passed through several ownerships during the 1870s before being destroyed by fire in 1877. An eight-year rebuild commenced that year before

Seek and you will find the Holy Grail, tucked away in Grace's Alley off Cable Street, in London's East End and within easy walking distance of the Tower of London. The boy Marie Lloyd loved may be up there in the gallery…

the building was bought by the East End Mission of the Methodist Church.

In the 30 years that Wilton's was a music hall, many of the best-remembered acts of early popular entertainment performed there, from George Ware, who wrote 'The Boy I love is up in the gallery', to Arthur Lloyd and George Leybourne ('Champagne Charlie'), two of the first music hall stars to perform for royalty. Wilton's was modelled on many other successful London halls of the time, including the second Canterbury Hall (1854).

Wilton's remains as a unique example of early music hall in England and Wales. In its heyday a 'sun-burner' chandelier of 300 gas jets and 27,000 cut crystals illuminated the mirrored hall. The hall had had space for supper tables, a benched area, and promenades around the outside for standing customers.

Wilton's was scheduled for demolition in the 1960s, but fortunately a campaign was started to save the building with support from people such as Sir John Betjeman, Peter Sellers and Spike Milligan. Wilton's was bought by the Greater London Council, which preserved it until 1999 when it was leased to Broomhill Opera Company until 2004. In June 2007 the World Monuments Fund added the building to its list of the world's '100 most endangered sites'. Wilton's Music Hall Trust took over ownership in 2004, and after a protracted period of restoration the building is now in good shape. Today the venue presents an eclectic range of cultural events and occasional re-enacted traditional music hall.

The Britannia Panopticon Music Hall, Glasgow

Along with Wilton's, the Britannia Panopticon is one of the oldest remaining music halls in Britain, and is now located above an amusement arcade at 113-117 Trongate, Glasgow.

First built in 1857 by Thomas Gildard and Robert H. M. MacFarlane, the

The elegant classical design of the front of Glasgow's Britannia music hall, which has hosted some of the biggest names on the circuit. Notably, in 1906 Stan Laurel made his first stage appearance here during an amateur night.

Panopticon was one of the first buildings in Glasgow to be powered by electricity in 1896, and became one of the first cinemas in Scotland during 1896.

Around 1860 the music hall was likely to have occupied the first and second floors of the building. However, it probably reached its final form in 1869, with a staircase entry from the ground floor vestibule opening onto Trongate. The first floor of the building would have once been the stalls level of the Britannia's auditorium.

The building went through many upgrades and alterations through the years.

In 1906 A. E. Pickard bought the building and changed its name to the Panopticon, a word meaning 'to view everything', derived from the Greek words 'pan', meaning 'everything', and 'opti', meaning 'to see'.

Under Pickard's management (1906-38), the Panopticon offered a variety of entertainments, such as amateur nights, the exhibition of animals, film shows (interspersed with live acts), the showing of sporting events films, clog-dancing competitions, and boxing demonstrations.

To this day the stalls and a horseshoe balcony accommodate the audience.

The Panopticon is currently being conserved by a trust that regularly performs traditional shows in the auditorium. *Photos courtesy of Debbie McCall with grateful help from Judith Bowers*

The Britannia Panopticon closed in 1938 and was hidden above a false ceiling. It was sold to a tailor and converted to a workshop. However, following the removal of the false ceiling in 2003, the Panopticon opened once more, and is now protected as a Category 'A' listed building.

City Varieties Music Hall, Leeds
Between 1953 and 1983 the famous City Varieties Music Hall, Leeds, achieved national fame as the venue for the BBC television programme *The Good Old Days*. The series very successfully recreated the Victorian music hall with a credible Chairman, Leonard Sachs, presenting many doyens of variety and lesser-known performers.

The Leeds City Varieties is a Grade II* listed music hall built in 1865 as an adjunct to the White Swan Inn (dating from 1748) in Swan Street, and the original interior is largely unaltered. It is a unique example of a mid-Victorian music hall. The interior is a long rectangle, with boxes separated by cast-iron columns along the sides at circle level.

The theatre was founded by local pub landlord and benefactor Charles Thornton and was originally called 'Thornton's New Music Hall and

Nine great British music halls and variety theatres

The venerable Chairman, Leonard Sachs, in fine form at Leeds City Varieties. *Courtesy of Bob Gregson*

Leeds City Varieties Music Hall. *Courtesy of Leeds Grand Theatre and Opera House Ltd*

Fashionable Lounge', which succeeded a 'singing room' above the inn. The name was subsequently changed to the White Swan Varieties, then Stansfield's Varieties, before becoming the City Palace of Varieties. Marie Lloyd, Charlie Chaplin and Houdini are among the artists who performed there.

The City Varieties was granted Heritage Lottery funds to help with major refurbishment and restoration, for which the theatre closed in January 2009, reopening in September 2011. The theatre now seats 467, and the sides of the balcony are closed to the public, providing space for additional lighting.

The music hall still presents live 'Good Old Days' performances over three weekends in the spring and four in the autumn, as well as pantomime and a regular programme of stand-up comedy and music concerts.

The BBC series *The Good Old Days* ran for 30 years. It authentically recreated the music hall for the modern audience, and one of the regular exponents of the music hall brand of comedy at City Varieties was Sir Ken Dodd. Northern comedy had its origins in music hall and it is therefore fitting to give this tribute.

Sir Kenneth Arthur Dodd OBE (8 November 1927-11th March 2018) was a Liverpool comedian, singer-songwriter, ventriloquist and actor, identified by his unruly hair and protruding teeth, his famous blue feather 'tickling stick' and his upbeat greeting of 'How tickled I am!' As a master of innuendo he would say to a woman seated in the front stalls, 'Have you ever been tickled, missus? This isn't television – you can't turn me off!'

Sir Ken was the last authentic vaudevillian, and was known for manipulating his audience into submission for more than 5 hours, with quick-fire gags and making his entrance on stage banging on a huge bass drum. As a ventriloquist

he introduced 'Dicky Mint'. Certainly his act embraced all of the elements of music hall performance from circus-clown-inspired acts, ventriloquism and comedy to serious tenor vocalist. He also created the characters of the 'Diddy Men', played by children.

Ken Dodd got his big break at the age of 26 when, in September 1954, he made his professional show-business debut as 'Professor Yaffle Chucklebutty, Operatic Tenor and Sausage Knotter' at the old Nottingham Empire. Ken loved the theatre and was instrumental in saving Blackpool's glorious Grand Theatre, the Palace Theatre at Manchester, and the Royal Court Theatre, Liverpool, after all three went dark in the 1970s. Doddy regularly played the Blackpool pier theatres from the 1950s and the Opera House for six seasons up to 1981. He also regularly played the Blackpool Grand up to his death, and once told me it was one of his favourite theatres. It was his aim to play all the major theatres of Britain and he continued to tour the UK with *The Ken Dodd Happiness Show* before pulling out of his tour in 2018 due to ill health. Sir Ken died at his home in Knotty Ash, Liverpool, on Monday 11 March 2018. Doddy was of the stock of northern music hall performers who learned their trade in the variety theatres as distinct from television, and in my view he was without doubt the last of the genre of traditional music hall comics, representing the end of an era.

Pavilion Theatre of Varieties, Glasgow

The Pavilion opened as a music hall at the corner of Renfield Street and Renfrew Street on 29 February 1904, and remains the last stronghold of a long music hall tradition in Glasgow. Little altered and virtually unspoilt since its inception, the seating capacity of 1,449 is made up of 677 in the stalls, 341

Above and right: This Victorian variety theatre has been fully restored. The grand theatrical styles incorporate art deco stained glass, rococo plasterwork, marble mosaic flooring, and Louis XV-style furnishings. *Courtesy of Marie Donnelly*

in the circle, 413 in the balcony and 18 box seats.

The Pavilion Theatre is now the only privately run theatre in Scotland and one of a few unsubsidised independent theatres left in Britain. Defying all the odds, it regularly purveys variety to this day, so it is all the more remarkable that it manages to survive.

With its imposing period terracotta facade, the

Top: The King of Knotty Ash. The photo is signed by Ken Dodd 'For Dorothy and David' and remains as a personal souvenir. *Author's collection*

Above: Ken Dodd on Blackpool's Comedy Carpet. *Courtesy of Gordon Young and Why Not Associates*

Nine great British music halls and variety theatres

Pavilion Theatre of Varieties was designed by Bertie Crewe in the grand manner for Thomas Barrasford. Performances in the early days were mainly variety, melodrama and pantomime. All the eminent music hall worthies turned up at the Pavilion at some time or other, including Marie Lloyd, Little Tich, Harry Lauder, Florrie Forde, Will Fyffe, Sarah Bernhardt and a then unknown Charlie Chaplin. Lulu (real name Marie Lawrie) broke box office records in 1975. Billy Connolly and other famous names rendered their own characteristic humour while Scottish songstresses Lena Zavaroni, Sheena Easton and Lena Martell were very popular with Pavilion audiences. A strong pantomime tradition was established in the 1930s and continues to this day.

During 1981 there was the prospect of closure after the Pavilion incurred heavy financial losses, just like its illustrious predecessors the Queens, Metropole, Empire, Alhambra and Empress theatres. Happily the old Pavilion was rescued by James Glasgow and transformed into a modest profit-maker with smash-hit shows, pantomime and one-night gigs. A policy of providing the best in live entertainment has been pursued consistently. The signs look good for the vibrant Pavilion Theatre of Varieties and, believe me, it is well worth a visit.

The King's Theatre, Edinburgh

The King's Theatre was built in 1905 by Edinburgh builder William Stewart Cruikshank, and opened in 1906 with a performance of *Cinderella*.

The interior decor is very ornate, with nine boxes on either side of the

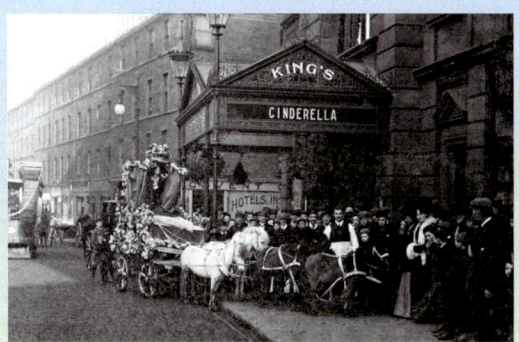

Top: The King's Theatre, Edinburgh, was built in 1905 and opened the following year with a performance of Cinderella, seen here with with promotional ponies and carriage.
Courtesy of Capital Theatres

Above: The theatre had a splendid Victorian auditorium. Initially the programming was undertaken under contract by Howard & Wyndham, whose company managed a chain of theatres in Britain, rivalling Moss Empires.

Above and right: The Kings Theatre originally had stalls and three circles – dress, family and gallery. The gallery was uncomfortable and latterly unsafe and was removed in the 1950s, reducing the theatre to three levels. The present seating capacity is 1,350.
Courtesy of Capital Theatres

proscenium. The King's Theatre was built as a variety theatre and has a long tradition of pantomime, with such stars as Stanley Baxter, Rikki Fulton and Jimmy Logan.

Following its recent refurbishment, the venue is even more majestic and imposing than ever. The foyer is wonderfully ornate with a semi-art nouveau feel, adding to a sense of occasion.

Gaiety Theatre, Ayr
The Ayr Gaiety was built in 1902, but was reconstructed after a fire in 1904. The theatre saw several years as a cinema after the First World War.

From 1925 to 1973 the theatre was run by the Popplewell family, and in later years, while owned and run by South Ayrshire Council, it remained the premier theatre in south-west Scotland. Over its long life the variety stage has seen performances from comedians, singers, variety acts and icons such as Sir Harry Lauder, Ken Dodd, Dave Willis, Jack Milroy and Gaiety legend Johnny Beattie. But financial pressures saw the Gaiety bow out on 31 January 2009.

In October 2012 Ayr Gaiety Partnership Limited took on a 99-year lease of the theatre for a 'peppercorn' rent from South Ayrshire Council. The theatre raised the curtain again on 11 December 2012 with the panto *Cinderella*, which turned out to be a sell-out run.

The new Ayr Gaiety is unlike most

theatres in the UK because it is largely run through voluntary effort. Although the volunteering effort overall is led by the Executive Director and Board, each volunteer team is supported and led by one of the staff team members.

As Scotland's first learning theatre with the University of the West of Scotland, the aim is to develop and promote in Ayrshire the value and role of the performing arts. The Gaiety is a Category B listed performing arts venue.

Liverpool's Empire Theatre

The huge Liverpool Empire Theatre is the second to be built on the site, and was opened in 1925. It has the largest two-tier auditorium in Britain and can seat 2,348 people. During its time it has hosted many genres of entertainment styles and historically music hall and variety. The theatre has hosted two Royal Variety Performances.

The first theatre on the site opened on 15 October 1866 and was named the 'New Prince of Wales Theatre and Opera House'. In 1896 the theatre was sold to Messrs Moss and Thornton for £30,000 and renamed 'The Empire'. This theatre closed on 16 February 1924, and was demolished.

The original Empire was replaced by the present larger theatre, which opened on 9 March 1925, designed by W. and T. R. Milburn for Moss Empires. The opening production was *Better Days*, starring Stanley Lupino, Maisie Gay and Ruth French. By

Left and above: The Ayr Gaiety is a former music hall serving south-west Scotland. *Courtesy of Guy Hicks Theatres*

Above, below left and below: The Empire Theatre, Liverpool. *Courtesy of Clare Jennings*

1977 the theatre was still owned by Moss Empires, which was making plans to dispose of it. Two years later it was acquired by Merseyside County Council and extensive renovation work was undertaken. The theatre underwent a further major refurbishment in 1999 with improved audience and stage facilities.

Many stars of the music hall graced the Empire's stage, and the list of international variety performers is awesome: Frank Sinatra, Judy Garland, Bing Crosby, Laurel and Hardy, Mae West, Charlton Heston, Roy Rogers and Trigger, the Carpenters, Tommy Steele, Bruce Forsyth, Morecambe and Wise, Ken Dodd, Shirley Bassey, Kylie Minogue, Elton John, Cilla Black, Chuck Berry, the Shadows and, of course, the Beatles, who appeared in the theatre on home ground during their early days. In addition, the theatre is reputed to be haunted by two ghosts who occasionally make guest appearances. The Empire now stages one-night stands, musicals, pop concerts, drama, ballet and opera. It is part of the Ambassador Theatre Group and is Grade II listed.

Palace Theatre, Manchester
The Palace and its sister theatre, the Opera House, in Manchester are operated by the Ambassador Theatre Group. The theatre was originally built as the Manchester Palace of Varieties and the genre of music hall and revue sustained it for decades. Known as the 'Grand Old Lady of Oxford Street', the Palace opened on 18 May 1891, having been designed by the architect Alfred Darbyshire and costing £40,500. The opening presentation, to a capacity audience, was the ballet *Cleopatra*; however, for several years it struggled to make a profit. Only when it broadened its scope and the building was made more attractive with popular performers did it become a resounding success.

Manchester's Palace Theatre is known as 'the Grand Old Lady of Oxford Street'. *Courtesy of Carole Pythian*

The theatre was redecorated and altered in 1896 to the designs of Frank Matcham, and he again worked on some improvements to the theatre in 1899. In 1913 the auditorium was again renovated by Bertie Crewe, and reopened with a reduced seating capacity of 2,600.

During the early part of the 20th century it came into its own as a variety theatre with music hall artists of the day, with stars such as Gracie Fields, Charles Laughton, Judy Garland,

Nine great British music halls and variety theatres

Noel Coward and Laurel and Hardy making appearances.

In September 1940 the theatre took a direct hit from a German bomb during the Manchester Blitz. However, the grand old lady's resilience led to her recovery, though she was seriously damaged. Moss Empires took over the ownership of the theatre in the early 1950s, and it continued to present variety and revue.

However, in the 1970s audience numbers declined, as they did in many live venues, and the Palace was threatened with closure. Fortunately it survived again to undergo a major refurbishment, restoring the auditorium and front of house to their Edwardian splendour and improving backstage facilities. With its large, well-equipped stage and nearly 2,000 seats, the theatre is a must-visit venue for major West End shows.

The Grade II listed building is now one of the best equipped and popular theatres outside London. It hosts the foremost touring musicals, often with major celebrities, and performances of opera and ballet together with various other comedy acts and one-night concerts.

The Alhambra Theatre, Bradford

Through the heyday of variety and up to the present day, the Alhambra Theatre has had a wonderful and varied history. This jewel in Bradford's crown was the vision of Francis Laidler, a local impresario. The Alhambra was officially opened at 2.00pm on 18 March 1914, and five days later it opened its doors to the general public for a variety show, which ran for a week.

The venue seats 1,400 people and is a popular choice for major touring companies. It remains an iconic venue, attracting the very best in star names and live entertainment to the city of Bradford.

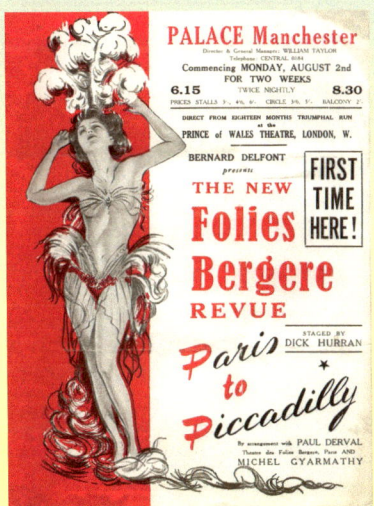

The New Folies Bergere Revue, no less, is billed at the Manchester Palace on 2 August 1954. *Author's collection*

Above: The Alhambra Theatre, Bradford, hosts the best in large-scale entertainment from international dance to musicals, drama and Yorkshire's biggest panto.

Right: A variety bill for the Alhambra featuring Jimmy Clitheroe. *Courtesy of Kevin O'Connor, Marine Lake Cafe, Southport*

Chapter Thirteen – A potpourri of comic railway interludes

On Britain's Edwardian streets horse-drawn carriages gave way to the petrol-driven motor cars that were beginning to revolutionise transport. In urban and rural areas traction engines were superseding horses for agricultural use and the haulage of heavy materials. Meanwhile the music halls regularly featured twice-nightly performances where comedy was a vital part of the repertoire, and stories concerning the early railways would not have been out of place.

It was the Railway Regulation Act of 1844 that required all companies to provide at least one train a day consisting of 3rd Class covered accommodation, travelling at not less than 12 miles per hour, for which the rate was not to exceed 1 penny a mile. Nevertheless, as late as 1868 passengers were still travelling in open 3rd Class carriages and, being exposed to the elements, took their umbrellas with them.

Victorian safety parallels archetypal incidents throughout the country. The diversity of accident causes ranged from jumping or falling off wagons and brake and signal failure, to animals and inebriated men on the tracks. A contemporary leaflet, 'Rules for Railway Travelling', provided general advice to the first Victorian travellers: 'If a 2nd Class carriage, as sometimes happens, has no door, passengers should take care not to put out their legs. Beware of yielding to a sudden impulse to spring from the carriage to recover your hat, which has blown off, or a parcel that has been dropped.'

From old asthmatic engines to bovines and boas – 1849

The 7-mile-long Preston to Longridge branch line opened on 1 May 1840 as a means of conveying large blocks of ashlar stone quarried at Longridge.

Seven years later the carriage of passengers seems to have been of secondary importance, with at least one passenger witnessing bizarre happenings and an apparent lack of investment on the line, with first-class bovines and 1st Class passengers sharing the same compartment. A ceaseless watch for boa constrictors had to be maintained, as anything could happen in this wildlife habitat. If this was an example of 1st Class travel, what was travel like in 3rd Class carriages during the late 1840s/'50s? *See letter below.*

'On Wednesday last I took it in my head to visit Longridge. I scrambled into a carriage, 1st Class of course, when to my surprise I found a quadruped in the shape of a fine calf, stretched within the compartment. Several other passengers noticed the same, but were given to understand that the practice was a common one, the Longridge

The Victorians travelled everywhere by train, even to outlandish resorts like Knott End, Lancashire. Perhaps there was life beyond the extremities of Knott End-on-Sea after all… *Courtesy of Bob Gregson*

A potpourri of comic railway interludes

Directors being no respecters of persons clean or unclean. Our journey, however, was not deficient in interest, for what with the wheezing puffs of the old asthmatic engine, the bleatings of the cow, and the imprecation of an old gentleman, whose juxtaposing with the calf appeared a grievous source of annoyance to him, we had music enough to spare. I had a deep veneration for the Longridge line, and therefore was extremely sorry to see so dirty and obnoxious a practice as that referred tolerated in the travelling arrangements. Would it be to too much to suggest that a separate box of some kind should be provided for the swine, etc, which are conveyed on this railway? If calves are to be located within a passenger carriage, why not cows; and if cows, why not bulls; and if bulls, why not the requisite accommodation for a rhinoceros or boa constrictor? The precedent is a dangerous one, and may grow into a great abuse.' [22]

Get out and push
The Preston historian, A. Hewitson, writing in 1883, did not speak too favourably about the original Preston North Union station of 1838, or of the first steam engines:

'At Preston the station was one of the most dismal, dilapidated, disgraceful-looking structures in Christendom. It was not only a very ill-looking, but an exceedingly inconvenient and dangerous station. The engines were said to be very small and the weak character of the old engines was such that often, when a heavy train was leaving Preston for the north, porters had to push at the side by way of assistance.'

Interesting reading, but it was no music hall joke! Furthermore, passengers had to cross the railway lines to reach other platforms. This dangerous procedure was finally ended when a footbridge was erected in 1855.

A one-way excursion ticket to the long drop
The precedent of the excursion train was to convey passengers to a predetermined destination and return with the benefits of travelling at reduced rates and with guaranteed income for the company. One of the most surreal excursion trains was arranged in 1849 when railway excursionists thronged to the scaffolds at Kirkdale Gaol, Liverpool, from as far away as London, to augment the large crowds gathered to watch the grim spectacle of two more public executions.

On 13 November 1849 Charles Dickens attended the public execution of Frederick and Maria Manning. The husband and wife were executed at the Horsemonger Lane Gaol, London, for the murder of their friend. Dickens was part of a crowd of 30,000 witnesses. The author denounced the public spectacle in a scathing letter to *The Times* newspaper. He claimed that he had attended the execution not to see the couple hanged, but to observe the crowd, which he described in some detail, as 'thieves, low prostitutes, ruffians, and vagabonds of every kind' whose 'foul behaviour' in jeering at the condemned and exhibiting shameless and 'brutal mirth' made him ashamed to be among their number.

The railways were used to convey passengers to witness all types of entertainment in Dickens's day. The ultimate deterrent was a macabre public spectacle, though unfortunately the staged executions were not as quick as the dropping of the tabs at the George Concert Hall. Before the railways and music hall the public spectacle of an execution had been one form of lawful entertainment for centuries, appealing to a merciless crowd of onlookers.

The new Metropolitan line into Farringdon, London, serving Newgate Prison, opened in 1863, and was always crowded with passengers on the day of public hangings. After all, to the mobs wanting a good view of the gallows it probably made a scene change from the local music hall gigs. One multiple hanging in 1864 saw five men killed in quick succession before a huge crowd of 20,000. The last public hanging took place outside Newgate Prison on 26 May 1868. Thereafter the bizarre entertainment spectacle was discontinued.

'I have lost my engine boss – it disappeared down a hole'

The first railway engineers had to overcome the problem of primitive locomotives being devoid of power, by constructing railways on level firm ground to minimise gradients. Steam locomotives could not cope with steep gradients and accordingly thousands of viaducts, bridges, tunnels, embankments and cuttings dotted the landscape of Britain. Nevertheless engines still ran out of steam, and one particular engine on the Furness Railway, working near Lindal Tunnel, disappeared altogether!

This disappearing act occurred at the height of the music hall era on 22 September 1892, and the key to solving the trick was subsidence. On that day 0-6-0 locomotive No 115 was quietly engaged in shunting a few quarry wagons when the earth beneath the engine suddenly parted company with the track. On seeing some rather ominous cracks precipitously appearing in the ground, the crew managed to leap from the footplate. The locomotive toppled over the brink with a one-way ticket into the vast hole, where it remains for eternity as a relic of railway heritage, albeit 200 feet below the surface of the earth at Lindal. The driver subsequently reported the matter to his superiors and the police, to whom he explained, 'I seem to have lost my engine but at least it was given a decent burial.' RIP No 115.

In 1892 FR 0-6-0 No 115 disappeared down a mine shaft while shunting at Lindal and is entombed in its subterranean tomb in perpetuity.
Cartoon by David Eaves

'Blow the whistle now – we've supped up'

Harry Clegg, whose forebears helped to re-form the Longridge Brass Band as the St Lawrence's Brass Band in 1883, recalled a through excursion train in 1908. The following demonstrates how the Longridge branch was used by the musicians for entertainment, not to mention the partaking of alcohol:

'Whit Monday 1908 was a wonderful day for us. It was a full train that left Longridge at 5.00am that sunny Whit-Monday morning. Travel in those days was limited and going to North Wales was something of an expedition to local people. I remember the train coming to a halt at a Welsh wayside station, and the stationmaster announcing that the engine had broken down, and it would be at least an hour before a relief got through. Some of the male passengers were soon paying a visit to the nearest pub. The stationmaster kindly promising that the engine driver would blow his whistle when it was time to go. Back in half the time, one of the men told the stationmaster: "Blow the whistle now – we've supped up." The lovely castle and fine buildings of Caernarvon delighted everyone, but the band needed more practice before going to the contest. Putting all they knew into a selection of sea shanties, the Longridge Band won first prize, their bandmaster, Mr Jack Clayton, receiving a silver cup, which was to become his own property in 1910.'[23]

The Whittingham Hospital Railway – a music hall conundrum

The Preston to Longridge and Whittingham branch lines symbolised the rural railways of bygone Lancashire in a forgotten scenario of quaint little trains in a vanishing natural landscape. During those halcyon days of the 1940s and 1950s, and long before digital television, mobile phones and satellite installations, it was funny old trains that helped to characterise the landscape, and who could resist boarding the train at Grimsargh's quaint branch-line station for a free ride to Whittingham?

The unique Whittingham line was constructed between 1887 and 1889 as a mineral line to convey coal, provisions and staff to the new asylum. The Whittingham train, known as the nurses' special, once ranked as one of the most fascinating and antiquated Victorian steam railways in the country. Furthermore, it claimed to be the only free passenger railway in the world, and anyone could travel as often as they liked.

During the early 1950s Grandfather Bowman first introduced me to the delights of the Whittingham line by taking me to Grimsargh on his BSA Bantam.

First impressions were that the steam locomotives and stock operating on the totally eccentric Whittingham railway made the veteran steam locomotives on the neighbouring Longridge branch line look like today's 'Eurostar'!

At Grimsargh I stood in awe at the sight of a truly antiquated steam engine named *James Fryars* and witnessed the early shift of hospital workers slamming the doors of three green carriages, which had been converted from LNWR guards vans by the hospital's joiners. On boarding the Whittingham train, suddenly and unannounced there was a jolt and a lurch, followed by a blow on the engine's whistle, as the train eased away from the platform to commence the journey to Whittingham. The patented coaches even had the luxury of wooden seats around the sides of the carriage and gas central-heating provided by a Calor Gas bottle, which was locked away inside the coaches. The 6-minute journey to Whittingham was a fairly comfortable ride, at a speed of around 15-20 miles per hour; the carriages had no continuous brakes.

From Grimsargh station the line curved in a north-westerly direction away from the Longridge line, alongside a siding before being reduced to a single track. The train then entered a cutting about 30-40 feet deep, gloriously festooned with colourful wild flowers. There was not a single bridge over the Whittingham line, only occupation/footpath crossings. As the train trundled along it seemed to acquire an alarming swaying motion while negotiating a left-hand curve on a high embankment. Approaching Whittingham station, the engine driver eased off the throttle and the train quietly clanked into the station without further incident.

As in most asylums, music played an important part in the life of patients, and the asylum had its own orchestra and brass band. Both staff and patients performed in full-scale stage productions including ad hoc music hall performances throughout the 20th century. The diminutive train that slowly crossed the level crossing in front of St Luke's main hospital building somehow completed the finishing touches to the staged music hall productions by patients and staff. It added to the allure of a remote establishment that seemed far apart from the 20th century. Here was a community that seemed to have been lost in the backwoods, when the railway was its only contact with the outside world, and when patients and staff began to discover that perhaps there was life beyond the gates of Whittingham after all! Today only a small number of footpaths cross the trackbed, where a faint scar on the landscape serves as a legacy of the Whittingham Hospital Railway, which, for all its unique characteristics, I liken to something of a music hall conundrum.

Above: This Stroudley 'D1' 0-4-2, as Southern No 2357 *Riddlesdown*, is seen at Guildford on 3 September 1932. It was transferred to Whittingham in 1947. *Courtesy of H. C. Casserley*

Below: The 'D1' 0-4-2 is seen again on its arrival at Whittingham station with an enthusiasts' special on 1 May 1954. Today it would have been destined for the Bluebell Railway or the National Railway Museum. *Courtesy of R. H. Hughes, Manchester Locomotive Society*

Above: The boiler of the 'D1', which was renamed *James Fryars*. It is a great pity that this historic locomotive was scrapped. *Courtesy of Bob Gregson*

Below: A four-wheel vertical-boiler Sentinel shunter, named *Gradwell*, crosses Brabiner Lane on the approach to Whittingham station. *Courtesy of Dorron Harper*

Encore: 'There's just time for one more verse of "Down at the Old Bull and Bush",' followed by personal recollections

This chapter embraces a miscellany of memories that have stimulated research. I begin with Wakes Weeks and journeys by steam train during the 1950s, while using holiday runabout tickets enabling families such as ours to enjoy trips to the Lancashire holiday resorts and see a good variety show or attend a matinee performance at Blackpool Tower Circus. Having boarded the train at Preston we waited eagerly for the first glimpse of Blackpool Tower across the Fylde plain, then we knew that the holiday had really begun. On arrival we caught a traditional tram car to Blackpool Tower Zoo to see the famous Wallace, of 'Lion and Albert' fame as recited by Stanley Holloway. I was to be enthralled at the Tower Circus with its motley collection of elephants, tigers and lions, and laughed at the famous clowns Charlie Carolli and Paul. The Victorian Grand Theatre symbolised the architectural work of Frank Matcham and was then owned by the Blackpool Tower Company. In later years I was to be mesmerised by the splendour of the Grand, where I well remember seeing the summer farces of the 1950s and 1960s with Thora Hird, Freddie Frinton, Arthur Askey and Hylda Baker, with her 6ft 6in stooge Cynthia!

An 'X'-rated performance without a censor

I have it on good authority that the late-night train home from Blackpool was popular with over-amorous couples and was better known by certain young lovers as the 'passion wagon'. In those days trains using non-corridor stock had the carriage compartment lights dimmed for the duration of the journey. The signalman was conversant with what went on too, having a front seat in the 'gods' from his usual elevated domain. As the train left Blackpool Central along the direct Marton route to Kirkham, the compartment would be romantically dark until the train reached Preston, so anything could happen within the gaze of the ever-watchful signalman!

Trainspotting at the 'glass bridge', Preston

The first railways were crucial in

Time for a kiss and a cuddle – nothing's changed!
Courtesy of Bob Gregson

transforming the social and economic prosperity of the country's towns and villages, and the Preston & Longridge

An LMS Aspinall 3F 0-6-0 passes Ribbleton station with a Preston-bound goods train, circa 1923-30. *Courtesy of Bob Gregson*

Railway was no exception. From being knee high to a grasshopper at the long-disused Ribbleton station, within 100 metres of my home, I regularly watched the goods trains go by. For me the branch was the epitome of a rural branch line, despite its modest credentials.

Recalling those great days of steam, as a 12-year-old, I joined my fellow trainspotters on the so called 'glass bridge', which formerly connected the south end of Preston station with East Cliff and the Park Hotel. During the 1950s I was able to enjoy the grand finale of the age of steam when all manner of marvellous steam engines still dominated the railway network. They consisted of 'Duchess', 'Royal Scot', 'Britannia', 'Patriot' and 'Jubilee' express passenger locomotives. We nicknamed the various types of locomotives, not forgetting the somewhat antiquated 'Jinty' No 47472, unofficially dubbed *City of Preston*.

However, for me the ultimate experience was witnessing the power of the splendid 'Coronation' 'Pacifics', proudly hauling the prestigious 'Royal Scot' Anglo-Scottish non-stop service and other main-line passenger services.

From the bridge there was a good view of the main line and the East Lancashire line as well as activity on the Preston Docks branch. Two double-headed 'Super D' 0-8-0 ex-LNWR locomotives certainly struggled with a train of more than 30 wagons up the steeply curved 1 in 49 gradient of the dock branch tunnel. Moreover, the

'Royal Scot' Class No 46155 passes under the remains of the 'glass bridge' at Preston station. *Stan Withers*

whiff of steam, the staccato barks, hissing and puffing and plumes of white smoke from tired old LNWR locomotives bombarded all of one's senses, somewhat reminiscent of a smoking volcano emerging from the subterranean depths of Preston.

Long before the days of modern traction, I ventured onto the hallowed ground of Preston engine shed. What a filthy, oily, sooty yet fabulous place this really was, with engines such as Nos 49191 and 49196 on home ground, yet just yards away from their principal haunt on the line to

'There's just time for one more verse of "Down at the Old Bull and Bush", followed by personal recollections

'Jinty' No 47472 (nicknamed *City of Preston*) is on station pilot duties at Preston station in the mid-1960s. *Stan Withers*

'Coronation' Class No 46238 *City of Carlisle* is on the Up Slow south of Leyland with a southbound relief service, probably Carlisle-Euston, in the early 1960s. *Stan Withers*

Longridge. We ticked off row upon row of overpowering, simmering locomotives being prepared for the road before we were chased off by the shed foreman. Alas, a disastrous fire destroyed the engine shed on 28 June 1960, causing superficial damage to nine locomotives. This did not augur well for the future of these engines, as clearly their days were numbered under British Railways' modernisation proposals to phase out steam.

After the fire a lasting memory is seeing rows of withdrawn 'Patriots'. Feelings of powerlessness prevailed on seeing No 45443 *Home Guard* and 'Coronation' 'Pacific' No 46257 *City of Salford* awaiting their fate in the burned-out shed. Regrettably, there was to be no railway Valhalla for *Home Guard* or the once proud *City of Salford*. One would have preserved the lot if that had been possible, but this preceded the thrust of the preservation movement.

During the 1960s vast inroads were made into the massive fleet of the various classes of revered steam engines, of all shapes and sizes, which were given a one-way ticket

Left: The Preston shed fire caused superficial damage to nine locomotives, Nos 42945, 45150, 45675 (*Hardy*) 46161, 48414, 49104, 49196, 49396 and 73128.

Below: 'No 45543 parading for duty, Sir'! The once proud *Home Guard* lost this particular battle together with all its fellow 'Patriots' here lined up in Preston engine shed in about 1961. *Noel Machell*

to the scrapyard. Inevitably this heralded the closure of the last three remaining BR engine sheds, at Carnforth, Rose Grove and Lostock Hall, in August 1968. I look back with feelings of lost opportunities during the age of steam, notwithstanding the reincarnation of the new-build 'Patriot' that has been given the awesome name of *The Unknown Warrior*.

The Grand Finale: All stations to the music hall by steam-hauled trains

'Ladies and gentlemen, I now proudly present, for your utter unmitigated enjoyment and reminiscence, a fabulous photographic portfolio of period steam trains that once conveyed passengers to the music hall, variety theatres, legitimate theatres and opera houses of Britain. All were kindly masterminded by that doyen of the camera, Mr Peter Fitton.'

LNER 'Pacific' No 4472 *Flying Scotsman* is seen crossing Arnside Viaduct with a northbound 'Cumbrian Coast Express' excursion train to Ravenglass and Sellafield on 12 May 1990.

Left: Midland Railway 4P 4-4-0 Compound locomotive No 1000, double-heading with 'Jubilee' 4-6-0 No 5690 *Leander*, approaches Grange while heading the 'Cumbrian Coast Express', the 13.15 from Carnforth to Sellafield, on 5 May 1980.

Below: The preserved LNWR 2-4-0 No 790 *Hardwick* crosses Arnside Viaduct while holidaymakers and fishermen seem quite oblivious to this historic moment captured by Peter Fitton on 23 May 1976.

Right: Doncaster-shedded 'A1' 'Pacific' No 60156 *Great Central* was deputising for a failed 'Deltic' diesel when photographed hauling the southbound 'Flying Scotsman' express at Peterborough station on 2 June 1962.

Below: Nicely clean ex-GWR 'King' Class 4-6-0 No 6011 *King James I* is about to leave Leamington Spa General station with 1M16, a Paddington to Birkenhead express, on 17 March 1962, the final year in which these fine locomotives were in service.

Rebuilt 'Royal Scot' Class No 46112, formerly named *Sherwood Forester* was working 1T40, a special from Nottingham to Blackpool, when photographed near Salwick on Easter Monday, 23 April 1962.

All stations to the music hall by steam-hauled trains

Above: 'Princess Coronation' Class 'Pacific' No 46252 *City of Leicester* passes Euston coal sidings, near Leyland, with the 1.30pm Euston to Perth express on a sunny 25 April 1962. Note the M6 under construction.

Above right: The celebrated LNER 'A4' streamliner No 4468 *Mallard* is seen approaching the Furness and Midland Junction at Carnforth with a Grange to Leeds excursion in August 1988. This engine has gone down in history as the holder of the world speed record for steam locomotives of 125.88mph (202.58km/h).

Right: 6P 'Jubilee' Class No 45565 *Victoria* enters Preston station from the south with a Laisterdyke to Morecambe special train on 30 May, 1964.

Above: Stanier Class 5 No 44926 awaits departure from Preston with the 12.25pm Blackpool North to Liverpool Exchange train on 3 January 1964.

Above right: Stanier Class 5 No 45078 and Hughes 'Crab' No 42734 double-head the 4.00pm Blackpool Central to Manchester Exchange service past Skew Bridge, south of Preston, on 24 August 1963.

Right: With a good head of steam, 2-6-4 tank No 42456 passes Farington Curve Junction with the 12.20pm local service from Preston to Wigan on 4 April 1964.

All stations to the music hall by steam-hauled trains

Left: At Skew Bridge, south of Preston, on 26 August 1961, BR 'Clan' No 72001 *Clan Cameron* is at the head of a Liverpool to Glasgow express passenger train.

Below left: 'Royal Scot' Class No 46139 *The Welch Regiment* was photographed passing Skew Bridge, Preston, with a morning Manchester to Blackpool train on 1 August 1962.

Below: Another 'Royal Scot' locomotive, No 46165 *The Ranger (12th London Regt)* has left Preston with the 15-coach southbound 'Lakes Express', seen here at Skew Bridge also on 1 August 1962. The crew will certainly need to work hard all the way to London!

Right: Gresley 'V2' 2-6-2 No 60828 leaves York with the 'Scarborough Flyer' from King's Cross on Saturday 10 August 1963.

Below: Bearing the chalked inscription 'STEAM FOR EVER', 'A4' No 60008 *Dwight D. Eisenhower* heads the daily Glasgow to King's Cross express at Rossington, south of Doncaster, on 15 June 1963, the last day of steam working into King's Cross. Today the locomotive is preserved in the USA.

Below right: Class 'A3' No 60105 *Victor Wild* is seen on the Down Fast line at Doncaster station with the northbound 'Northumbrian' from King's Cross to Newcastle on 15 April 1961.

Above: On the last day of regular steam into King's Cross, 'A3' Class No 60088 *Book Law* heads the up 'Northumbrian' at Rossington, south of Doncaster, on 15 June 1963.

Right: Newton Heath-shedded Class 5 No 44735 arrives at Morecambe Promenade station with 1T54, a day excursion from Colne, on 28 July 1963.

Far right: Deputising for a diesel, 'Coronation' 'Pacific' No 46237 *City of Bristol* arrives at Lancaster Castle with the 09.25am Crewe to Perth express on 19 May 1964.

Above: 'Jubilee' No 45666 *Cornwallis* heads south with the 'Lakes Express' at Bolton-le-Sands, south of Carnforth, on 29 July 1963.

Above right: GWR 'Castle' Class No 7000 *Viscount Portal* passes Reading with the 'Cheltenham Spa Express' to Paddington on 22 August 1961.

Right: Fresh from overhaul at Crewe Works, 'Coronation Pacific' No 46242 *City of Glasgow* is seen heading the down 'Red Rose' express at Kilsby, south of Rugby, on 23 May 1962.

All stations to the music hall by steam-hauled trains

Left: Collett-designed Great Western Railway 4-6-0 No 6026 *King John* is seen working a Paddington to Shrewsbury train through West Ruislip on 18 August 1961.

Below left: On 2 June 1962 'A3' 'Pacific' No 60082 *Neil Gow* has stopped at Peterborough on the Leeds to King's Cross 'White Rose' express.

Below: The now preserved Class 'A3' No 60103 *Flying Scotsman* arrives at King's Cross from Leeds on 21 August 1961.

Above left: At Martholme Crossing north of Peterborough on the East Coast Main Line, Gresley 'A3' No 60112 *St Simon* is heading an express towards London King's Cross on 16 June 1962.

Left: Rebuilt 'Battle of Britain' Class 'Pacific' No 34050 *Royal Observer Corps* is seen passing Raynes Park station with the 11.30 express from Waterloo to Bournemouth on 1 July 1965.

Above: LMS Stanier Class 5 No 44691 is seen working inter-regional holiday train 1X37 to Bournemouth near Worting Junction on the old Southern Railway on Saturday 21 July 1962.

Right: 'Jubilee' Class No 45721, formerly named *Impregnable*, was photographed passing Spen Lane signal box near Salwick with the 12.27 Liverpool Exchange to Blackpool North train on 1 September 1965.

Above: GWR 'Manor' Class No 7819 *Hinton Manor* has charge of the down 'Cambrian Coast Express', leaving Shrewsbury for Aberystwyth on a dull 21 July 1964.

All stations to the music hall by steam-hauled trains

Below: BR 'Britannia' Class 'Pacific' No 70027, formerly named *Rising Star*, has charge of a Leeds to Blackpool North excursion on Easter Monday, 27 March 1967. The photo was taken as the train neared the closed Euxton ROF station on the now electrified Bolton to Preston line.

Above: Passengers look out as Horwich 'Crab' No 42700 rounds the curve from Morecambe South Junction to Bare Lane with 1T69, a day excursion from Rochdale to Morecambe, on 28 July 1963. Such trains were to cease running soon afterwards as more people acquired cars; however, the locomotive survived into preservation.

Left: Very clean 'Jubilee' No 45635 *Tobago* hauls 1X50, an Illuminations Special from Doncaster to Blackpool Central, along the 1903 Marton line at Plumpton on 29 September 1962. The line was closed in the late 1960s, with no trace now remaining.

The attractive old wooden farm bridge at Eastham, between Moss Side and Lytham, is shown in this picture of 'Black 5' No 45118 working the 3.10pm Manchester to Blackpool Central stopping train on 27 July 1963. The mixed set of coaches was typical of the period. The bridge was demolished not long afterwards.

Appendix One – Historiography

With certain exceptions the coverage of Edwardian music hall outside London is relatively understudied, and the growth and decline of Preston's Victorian and Edwardian music hall industry has not been the subject of previous academic research. The present author's case study alluded to in *From a Gin Palace to a King's Palace*, discovers the origins and development of Preston music hall within the period c1840-1914 and offers comparisons with existing studies while demonstrating how it was a microcosm of music hall growth and illustrating how far Preston had its own unique characteristics.

In the introduction to *Music Hall: The Business of Pleasure*, Bailey reviews several different approaches to music hall history. He shows how social historians have become interested in the halls, viewing them as part of working-class culture but within a capitalist society, so that its development from pothouse to palace is represented as 'a product of conflict rather than consensus'[24] Opposition to the pub music hall, particularly from temperance campaigners, was important in shaping Victorian and Edwardian variety theatres.

Bratton debates the culture of music hall itself by focussing upon class, gender and the songs and sketches that made up the music hall repertoire.[25]

Kift marks an important stage in the writing of music hall history. She notes that up to her study the focus of interest has been almost exclusively on the London halls. Kift considers which classes of people composed audiences at different times during the evolution of music hall. Her interest also extends to the degree of success of social reformers and how far working-class people were able to espouse for themselves respectable values like family life and self-improvement.[26] Kift's work is also based on case studies of Bolton, Leeds, Glasgow, Liverpool, Sheffield and Manchester.

One particularly important local study is Poole's work on Bolton, which examines music hall as part of a growing leisure industry. As well as discussing the influence of respectability, he considers how, as music hall developed and as economic circumstances improved, it began to attract a wider audience. These consisted of relatively well-off shopkeepers and assistants, skilled workers and clerks. An additional significant aspect of his work is the link he explores between circus and music hall.[27]

Reid's findings on the legitimate theatre in Birmingham are helpful as a guide in the discussion of audiences and competition between the genre of theatre and music hall. The legitimate theatre offering Shakespeare and melodrama as well as music hall was popular with the working classes in both towns, and the pit and gallery segregated audiences, although it would probably be an overconfident assumption to conclude that higher-priced tickets always attracted the upper classes.[28]

Appendix Two – Frank Matcham's great British theatres

Listed below are the significant theatres of Frank Matcham, with those that still stand, whole or in part, shown in bold. It has been taken from the Theatres Trust's 'Guide to British Theatres 1750-1950, A Gazetteer'.

1873 Paignton, Oldway House Theatre
1879 London Elephant and Castle Theatre
1885 Glasgow, Hengler's Grand Cirque
1885 Glasgow, Royalty
1887 Brighton, Grand
1888 Bolton, Theatre Royal
1888 Stockport, Theatre Royal
1888 Brighton, Alhambra
1888 Newcastle-upon-Tyne, Alhambra
1888 Middlesbrough, Royal
1888 London Woolwich Grand, unexecuted
1889 Blackpool, Opera House
1889 St Helens, Theatre Royal
1889 Halifax, Grand
1889 Bury, Theatre Royal
1891 Ashton-under-Lyne, Theatre Royal
1891 Portsmouth, New Prince's
1891 **Cheltenham, Everyman Theatre**
1891 Southport, Opera House
1892 **Edinburgh, Empire now Festival Theatre**
1892 Llandudno, Victoria Palace, unexecuted
1893 Hull, Grand
1894 **Blackpool, Grand Theatre and Blackpool Tower Ballroom and Tower Circus**
1894 Bolton, Grand
1894 **Wakefield, Royal Opera House**
1895 **Belfast, Grand Opera House**
1895 Sheffield, Empire
1895 Salford, Regent
1896 London, Brixton Borough Theatre
1896 Cardiff, Empire
1897 Hull, Empire Palace
1897 South Shields, Empire/Palace
1897 Glasgow, Empire
1898 Birmingham, Alhambra
1898 Great Yarmouth, Theatre Royal
1898 Leeds, Empire Palace
1898 Morecambe, Royalty
1898 Stoke-on-Trent (Hanley), Grand
1898 Nottingham, Empire Palace
1899 Huddersfield, Grand (project, never built)
1899 London, New Cross Empire
1899 **London, Richmond Theatre**
1899 Newport, Empire Palace
1899 Salford, Broadway
1900 **London, Hippodrome**
1901 **London, Hackney Empire**
1901 Leicester, Palace
1903 **Buxton, Opera House**
1903 **London, Shepherd's Bush Empire**
1903 **Harrogate, Royal Hall**
1903 London, Marlborough
1904 **Glasgow, King's**
1903 Newcastle-upon-Tyne, Empire
1904 Manchester, Ardwick Green Empire
1904 Manchester, Hippodrome
1904 **London, Coliseum**
1905 Glasgow, Coliseum
1905 Ipswich, Hippodrome
1905 **Liverpool, Olympia**
1906 **Aberdeen, His Majesty's**
1907 London, Willesden Hippodrome
1907 **Portsmouth, Southsea King's**
1909 London, Ilford Hippodrome
1910 London, Finsbury Park Empire
1911 Brighton, Alhambra Opera House
1911 London, Lewisham Hippodrome
1911 Glasgow, Olympia (facade)

1911 London, Winter Garden
1911 **London, Victoria Palace**
1912 Chatham, Empire
1912 London (Hounslow), Chiswick Empire
1912 **London, Wood Green Empire (facade remains)**
1912 **Bristol, Hippodrome**

Notes

1 *Preston Chronicle*, 14 September 1861
2 The 1901 Census shows circus artist Joseph Smith, 46 years, residing at 5 Fox St, Preston, with a wife and four children.
3 Clay, A. *Chaplain's Annual Report, Preston House of Correction, 1842* (L.R.O. QGR2/32 – 1842, p5)
4 Ibid
5 *Preston Chronicle*, 12 November 1864
6 *Preston Chronicle*, 10 December 1864
7 *Preston Chronicle*, 18 January 1865
8 *Preston Chronicle*, 26 November 1870
9 Earl, J. 'Building the Halls,' in Bailey *Music Hall* (Oxford University Press, 1986) p1
10 Honri, P. *Working the Halls* (Saxon House, 1973) p28
11 Walton, J. *Lancashire: A Social History* (Manchester University Press, 1987) p299
12 Clay, J. *Annual Report House of Correction* (L.R.O. QGR2/3/4 1850)
13 Crump, J. 'Provincial Music Hall in Leicester' in Bailey *Music Hall* (Open University Press, 1986) p53
14 Mander and Mitchenson, *British Music Hall* (London, 1966) p47
15 Kift, D. *Victorian Music Hall* (Cambridge University Press, 1996) p166
16 Anderson, M. *Family Structure in Nineteenth Century Lancashire* (Cambridge University Press, 1971) p24
17 Walton, J. *Lancashire: A Social History 1558-1939* (Manchester University Press, 1987) p199
18 Ibid
19 Russell, D. *Popular Music* (Manchester University Press, 1987) pp79-82
20 Documentation provided by Major A. Burt Briggs, April 1999
21 A fair at Hull had cinematograph tents from 1897. Reid, D. 'Playing and Praying', ed Daunton, M., *Cambridge Urban History* (Cambridge University Press, 2000) p760. Also Toulmin, V. 'We take them and make them', *Lost World of Mitchell and Kenyon* (British Film Institute, London 2004) p59
22 *Preston Guardian*, 1849
23 Clegg, Harry 'Bandsmen of Yesterday' (*Longridge News & Advertiser*, October 1968)
24 Bailey, P. *Music Hall: The Business of Pleasure* (Open University Press, 1986) ppxiii-xv
25 Bratton, *Music Hall Performance and Style* (Open University Press, 1986)
26 Kift, D. *The Victorian Music Hall* (Cambridge University Press, 1996) p3
27 Poole, R. *Leisure and Music Hall in Nineteenth Century Bolton* (Lancaster, 1982)
28 Reid, D. 'Popular Theatre in Victorian Birmingham' in *Performance and Politics in Popular Drama*, ed Bradby, D. (Cambridge University Press, 1980) pp65-85

Acknowledgements and Bibliography

I would like to thank Gary Morecambe for kindly writing such a nice Foreword, and Michael Fountain, who helped me with research into his former boss and friend, Eric Morecambe. Research has encompassed a wide range of primary sources. I acknowledge the help of staff at the National Archives, Kew, London; The Victoria and Albert Museum Theatre Library, London; National Railway Museum; Lancashire Archives; British Newspaper Library; Wikipedia and www.arthurlloyd.co.uk for sources of theatre clarification.

I am very grateful for the help and encouragement of Aidan Turner Bishop and Bob Gregson; to photographers Stan Withers, Peter Fitton and Noel Machell for their excellent photographs of steam locomotives; David Eaves for his technical help and photographs; and to many music hall and theatre staff for their time and patience in forwarding me a splendid portfolio of photographs of some of the most beautiful theatres in Britain.

I thank the late Major A. Burt Briggs who helped me with my research into Blackpool and Lancashire's entertainment industry. Also to journalists of long ago who wrote in local newspapers about the social impact of music hall and railways on local communities. I thank all contributors, while pointing out that I have made every effort to trace copyright owners of material and apologise for possible omissions.

Primary sources
National Archive, Kew, London

DT 31/3935/24925 *Music Hall Artists' Association*

Manuscripts held at the Lancashire Record Office
Plan of the Theatre Royal, 1898, PSPR2/224
Details of sales by auction of Broadhead's theatres 1932/33, DDX 74/16/70
Annual Reports of the Rev J. Clay, 1824-1858, QGR/2-3 to 42

Parliamentary Papers at the Lancashire Record Office
Further Report on the Licensing of Places of Public Entertainment, P.P. 1854, X1V
House of Commons Select Committee – Theatrical Licences and Regs. P.P.1866, XV1
1st Report, Select Committee, House of Lords, on Intemperance, P.P. 1877, X1

Newspapers and periodicals
The Era, 1838-1918
Lancashire Evening Post, 1886-1957

Oral interviews
Major A. Burt Briggs (direct descendant of W. H. Broadhead), 22 January 1998
John Baron, 4 March 1998
Leonard Rossiter, 19 December 1977
Jim Tattersall, 2 February 1998

Secondary sources

Anderson, M. *Family Structure in Nineteenth Century Lancashire* (Cambridge, 1971)
Bailey, P. *Music Hall: The Business of Pleasure* (Milton Keynes, 1986)

Acknowledgements and Bibliography

Bratton, J. *Music Hall Performance and Style* (Milton Keynes, 1986)
Bradshaw, G. *Railway Guide* (first published in 1863)
Clinker, C. R. *Railway History Sources* (AO4CC1)
Cunningham, H. *Leisure in the Industrial Revolution* (London, 1980)
Fountain, M. and Jenkinson, P. *Driving Mr Morecambe* (Authors on Line, 2013)
Henderson, W. *The Lancashire Cotton Famine* (Manchester, 1969)
Hindle, D. J. *Twice Nightly* (Preston, 1999)
   From a Gin Palace to a King's Palace (History Press, 2010)
   'All Stations to Longridge' (Amberley Publishing, 2010)
   Life in Victorian Preston (Amberley Publishing, 2014)
   Planes, Trains, Tramcars and Ships (Amberley Publishing, 2015)
   Enjoying the Cumbrian Coast railway (Silver Link Publishing, 2017)
Hunt, D. *History of Preston* (Preston, 1992)
Kift, D. *The Victorian Music Hall* (Cambridge, 1996)
Russell, D. *Popular Music in England 1840-1914* (Manchester, 1987)
Scott, H. *The Early Doors* (London, 1946)
Walton, J. *Lancashire: A Social History, 1558-1939* (Manchester, 1987)

Articles in books and journals

Crump J. 'Provincial Music Hall', in Bailey, P. *Music Hall* (Milton Keynes, 1986)
Cunningham, H. 'Leisure', ed Benson J. *The Working Class in England* (1985)
Earl, J. 'Building the Halls', in Bailey, P. *Music Hall* (Milton Keynes, 1986)
Russell, D. 'Varieties of Life: The making of the Edwardian Music Hall' in Booth, M. and Kaplan, J. *The Edwardian Theatre* (Cambridge 1996)

Index

Aberdeen, His Majesty's Theatre 53, 70-72
Accrington, New Hippodrome Theatre 100
Acts of Parliament: Factories Act, 1850 12; Metropolitan Management & Building Act, 1878 26; Preston Improvement Act, 1880 26; Railway Regulation Act, 1844 152; Theatres Act 1843 25
Allen, J. J. 76
Ambassador Theatre Group 65, 73, 150
Ayr, Gaiety Theatre 148-49

Baker, Hylda 9, 83, 97, 157
Barraclough, Roy 83
Barrasford, Thomas 147
Barrow-in-Furness, cinemas in 101
Bartholomew, Eric see Morecambe and Wise
Bartholomew, Sadie 85, 88, 93
Beale, Robert 55
Beatles 57, 102, 110
Belfast, Grand Opera House 53, 68-69
Bickerstaff, John 112
Black, George 59
Blackburn 41, 94, 100; theatres 100, 102
Blackoe, Edward 13
Blackoe, John 14
Blackpool 21, 107, 108; Comedy Carpet 115-16, 146; trams 23
Blackpool Piers: Central and Pavilion Theatre 114, 115, 118; North and Pavilion Theatre 114, 115, 118; South and Grand Pavilion/Pier Head/Regal Theatre 114, 117
Blackpool theatres: ABC 102, 110; Alhambra/Palace 112-13; Derby Baths 109; Grand 53, 56, 57-58, 115, 146, 157; Empire/Hippodrome 108, 109, 110, 117; Borough/Feldmans/Queen's 102, 111-12, 116; Palace 117; Tower, Ballroom and Circus 24, 52, 108, 112, 157; Winter Gardens/Pavilion/Opera House 110, 111, 113, 115, 116, 117
Bolton 11, 13; Star Music Hall 11
Braben, Eddie 91
Bradford, Alhambra Theatre 15
Brennan, Jimmy 111-12
Briggs, Major A. Burt 58
Brighton, Theatre Royal 29-30
Bristol, Hippodrome 23, 53, 66-68
Briton, James 17
Broadhead, Percy 'Sonny' 78, 83
Broadhead, William Birch 76
Broadhead, William Henry 16, 58, 76, 77, 79
Buffalo Bill's Wild West Show 11
Burnley 100; Empire, Victoria and Gaiety Theatres 100, 101
Bury 76
Bury St Edmunds, Theatre Royal 29
Butlin's holiday camps and reliance on railways 34-37
Butt, Sir Alfred 51
Buxton, Opera House 53, 65-66

Calcutt, Thomas 47
Caledonian Railway 19
Chairmen, music hall 11, 12, 14, 15, 144
Chaplin, Charlie 62, 72, 81, 145, 147
Chart, Henry John Nye 30
Circuses 10
Clay, Rev John 12
Clegg, Harry 154
Clitheroe, Jimmy 118, 151
Cody, William see Buffalo Bill
Cons, Emma 28
Cook, Thomas 17-18
Crazy Gang 59, 60, 61, 98
Crewe, Bertie 101, 147, 150
Cruikshank, William S. 147
D'Oyly Carte, Richard 46
Darbyshire, Alfred 150
Dickens, Charles 39-40, 42, 43, 153; *Hard Times* based on Preston 40
Dodd, Ken 56, 83, 90, 115, 118, 145-46, 148
Douglas (IoM), Gaiety Theatre 140-41; horse-drawn tramway 140

Eccles 33, 76; Lyceum Theatre 76
Edinburgh theatres: Empire/Festival 6, 53, 72, 91; King's 147-48
Elgar, Sir Edward 56, 57
English National Opera 75
Excursion trains 21; Bass Brewery 103, 104
Fields, Gracie 56, 65, 68, 95, 151
Fires in theatres, and accompanying legislation 26
Fleetwood 21, 107, 108
Forde, Florrie 97, 98, 103, 106, 147
Formby, George 68, 95, 96, 136
Forsyth, Bruce 60, 98, 113
Fountain, Michael (Eric Morecambe's driver) 91, 93
Furness Railway 17, 20, 32, 38, 101, 105, 107

Geoghegan, Mr 11
Gibbons, Walter 59
Gildard, Thomas 143
Glasgow theatres: Britannia Panopticon 143-44; Empire 77, 89, 90, 91, 98; King's 53, 72-73, Pavilion 6, 146-47
Glasgow, James 147
Great Lafayette, The 72
Great Vance, The 48, 49
Grimaldi, Joseph 50, 51
Grimsargh 155

Harris, Sir Augustus 46
Harrogate, Royal Hall (Kursaal) 52,

Index

53, 54-57
Hengler, Fredrick 59
Hesketh Bank 129
Hird, Thora 106, 157
Houdini, Harry 81-82, 145
Howard and Wyndham 76
Hume, Walter 78
Hundred End 134
Hylton, Jack 61, 85

Isle of Man, Gaiety Theatre 53
Isle of Man Railway 139
Isle of Man Steam Packet Co 138

James, Jimmy 83, 118
Jewel and Warriss 98, 109, 110

Kean, Edmund 27
Killigrew, Thomas 49, 50
King, Hetty 9, 56
Koringa and Friends 80-81

Laidler, Francis 151
Lancashire & Yorkshire Railway 103, 129, 130
Lancaster & Carlisle Railway 18
Lancaster, Grand Theatre 58
Land, David and Brook 30
Langtry, Lillie 56, 57, 65
Lashwood, George 22
Lauder, Harry 56, 147, 148
Laurel and Hardy 62, 65, 68, 72, 96, 151
Lee, Alfred 15
Leeds theatres: City Varieties 144-46; Grand 88; Princess Concert Hall 15
Leno, Dan 44, 56
Leybourne, George 15, 44, 143
Lightfoot, Douglas 140

Lindal 154
Little Tich 44, 46, 147
Littler, Prince 60
Liverpool & Manchester Railway 17, 20
Liverpool Overhead Railway 22
Liverpool, 76; theatres: Empire 22, 85, 86, 96, 97, 102, 149-50; Olympia 53; Pavilion 79, 112; Royal Court 9, 146
Llandudno, Pier Pavilion 21
Lloyd Webber, Andrew 49, 60
Lloyd, Arthur 143
Lloyd, Marie 7, 8, 43, 44, 46, 48, 56, 62, 65, 145, 147
London & North Western Railway 19, 20, 21, 32
London Midland & Scottish Railway 21, 32, 108; 'Coronation Scot' 34, 35
London theatres: Alhambra Music Hall 45, 46; Canterbury Hall 12, 42, 43, 46, 143; Coliseum 52, 59, 74-75; Eagle tavern 43; Empire, Leicester Square 45, 94; Finsbury Park Empire 98; Gaiety 45, 52; Hackney Empire 49, 52, 62-63, 97; Hippodrome 52, 59, 61-62; Lyric, Hammersmith 53; Metropolitan 42, 48, 49; Middlesex 43; New London 43, 48; Old Vic (Royal Victoria Hall) 27; Oxford Music Hall 43; Palace 47-48; Palace of Varieties 46, 47; Palladium 49, 52, 58-60, 88; Pavilion 44, 45; Royal English Opera House 46, 47; Royal Opera House 27, 75; Royal Standard 61; Talk of the Town 61; Theatre Royal 49-51, 60; Victoria Palace 49, 53, 59, 60-61; Wilton's 43, 142-43; Winter Garden 48
Longridge, Palace Cinema 94

Lostock Hall 130
Lumière, Auguste and Louis 45, 72, 94
Lune, Ted 83
Lytham 21

MacFarlane, Robert H. M. 143
McNaughten, Frank 101
Manchester 76; theatres: Ardwick Green Hippodrome 53-54; Grand Junction 76, 79; Hulme Hippodrome 76, 112; Metropole 76; Midland Hotel 24; Opera House 150; Palace 23, 146, 150-51; Royal Osborne 76; Theatre Royal 24
Manx Electric Railway 140
Manx Northern Railway 139
Matcham, Frank 49, 52ff, 74, 110, 134, 140, 141
Maxwell, James 112
Mazzei, Andrew 112
Meols Cop 130
Midland Railway 24, 105
Milburn, W. & T. R. 149-50
Modley, Albert 105
Morecambe 21, 96, 104; Bay 107; theatres: Alhambra 105; Royalty 106; Victoria Pavilion/Winter Gardens 76, 96, 105, 106
Morecambe and Wise, and as individuals 85ff, 98, 113, 118
Morecambe, Joan 91, 93
Morton, Charles 12, 43, 46
Moss Empires 52, 72, 76, 77, 88, 90, 98, 106, 149, 150
Moss, Sir Edward 52, 59, 76
Music Hall Artistes' Railway Association 37, 38
Music halls: first purpose-built 7; origin and development of 6, 10, 11, 12, 15,

31; definition 10; co-existing with railways 18-19, 31; denied permission to stage drama 25; rail concessions for artists 37-38; linked with alcohol 25; introduces cinema 94, 95; competition from other entertainment 97; decline of 6, 17

National Theatre 28
Nelson 102
Newcastle-upon-Tyne, Theatre Royal 53, 69-70, 98
Newsome's Circus 10-11
North Union Railway 39, 40, 153
Nottingham, Empire Theatre 146
Novello, Ivor 51

O'Connor, Des 90, 113
Onda, Will (Hugh Rain) 16, 94
Osborne, John 96, 99

Parnell, Val 60, 91
Pavarotti, Luciano 68
Penwortham 128, 129, 130, 131, 134
Pepys, Samuel 50
Phipps, Charles 30
Pickard, A. E. 144
Popular songs 14-15
Portsmouth, New Theatre Royal 53
Preston 13, 14, 16, 17, 39, 76, 83, 94, 97; Butler Street station 10-11, 130; engine shed 158, 160; Fishergate Hill station 128, 129, 130, 131; 'glass bridge' 157-58; Longridge branch line 152, 154; North End FC 15, 16, 82; population 41
Preston & Wyre Railway 107
Preston theatres: Albion Music/Concert Hall 12, 13, 26; Clarence

Music Hall 15; Empire 8, 9, 24, 33, 34, 83, 84, 99; Gaiety Palace Theatre of Varieties/Princes 15, 16, 99; George Concert Room/Music Hall 13, 15, 41; King's Head 41; King's Palace 17, 78, 79, 80, 81, 82, 83, 84, 91, 97, 99, 100; New King's Head Concert Hall 14; Palladium Cinema 95; Picturedrome 95; Public Hall 102 Royal Hippodrome 7, 16, 77, 78, 84, 97, 99, 100; Theatre Royal 10, 41, 99
Prostitutes, in music halls 16
Public houses, as places of entertainment 11, 13, 26; decline of 26
Pye, Harry 11

Rain, Hugh *see* Onda, Will
Randle, Frank 83, 98, 108, 113
Rawcliffe, G. B. 100
Richmond Theatre 53, 63-65
Robey, George 46, 83
Robinson, Joseph 52
Royal Variety Performances 48, 59, 60, 111, 149

Sachs, Leonard 144
Sadlers Wells Opera 74, 75
Safety curtain *see* fires
Salford, Royal Hippodrome 78
Sergenson, Thomas 57
Sharples, Thomas 11
Sheffield, Empire Theatre 90
Sheridan, Richard Brinsley 50
Sims, Ernest 77
Singing rooms/saloons 12, 13, 41, 145
Smith, Joseph 11
Southport 21, 102, 134; Chapel Street station 134, 137; railway line electrified 130; railway closed 137
Southport theatres: Garrick 134-137; Opera House 134, 135; Pier Pavilion 135
Southsea, Kings Theatre 53
Stage plays, definition of 25
Stockton & Darlington Railway 17
Stokes, Mervin Russell 141
Stoll, Sir Oswald 52, 59, 67, 74

Tattersall, Jim 89-90
Theatrical traffic on railways 32-33
Thornton, Charles 144
Tilley, Vesta 46, 56, 72, 83
Tonge, George 134
Trams 22-24
Tuke, Charles 112

Variety Artists Federation 37, 38
Variety theatre, definition of 10; supersedes music hall 17, 97; of London 44; decline of 98, 99, 102

Wakefield, Theatre Royal 66
Wakes Weeks 103, 104, 109, 157
Ware, George 143
West Lancashire Railway 128, 129, 130
Whitby 22
Whittingham Hospital Railway 155-56
Wigan 102, 112
Wilkins, William 29
Wilton, John 142
Winter, Mike and Bernie 90-91
Wiseman, Ernest *see* Morecambe and Wise
Wolverhampton, Grand Theatre 88
Wyatt, Benjamin Dean 50

Railway photographic locations
Arnside Viaduct 161, 162
Ballasalla 139
Bath Green Park 124, 125
Boat of Garten 33
Bolton Trinity Street 122
Bolton-le-Sands 170
Carnforth 165
Chester General 127
Coniston 32
Crossens 133
Doncaster 168, 169
Eastham 176
Euxton 175
Farington Curve Junction 120, 123, 166; Goods Yard 126
Grange-over-Sands 162
Hesketh Bank 133
Hoole 132
Keswick 33
Kilsby 170
King's Cross 171
Knott End 152
Lakeside, Windermere 32
Lancaster 77, 105, 169; Galgate 86
Leamington Spa 163
Leeds City 87, 121
Leyland 120, 159, 165
Longton Bridge 132
Lostock Hall 120, 125, 126
Manchester Central 122; Victoria 127
Meols Cop 133
Miles Platting 119
Morecambe Promenade 169; South Junction 175
New Longton & Hutton 132
Oswestry 121
Penwortham Cop Lane 128, 131
Peterborough 163, 171, 172
Plumpton 174
Preston 31, 123, 131, 137, 159, 160, 165, 166, 167
Raynes Park 172
Reading 170
Salwick 164, 173
Scarborough 104
Sheffield Victoria 122
Shrewsbury 173
Southport 137
Vauxhall 123, 124
Wakefield 121
West Ruislip 171
Whitehouse West Junction 130
Whittingham Hospital Railway 156
Worting Junction 172
York 168